DATE DUE

948.1
HEP   Hepso, Mike
             Norway

Morrill School Library
Chicago Public Schools
6011 S. Rockwell
Chicago, IL 60629

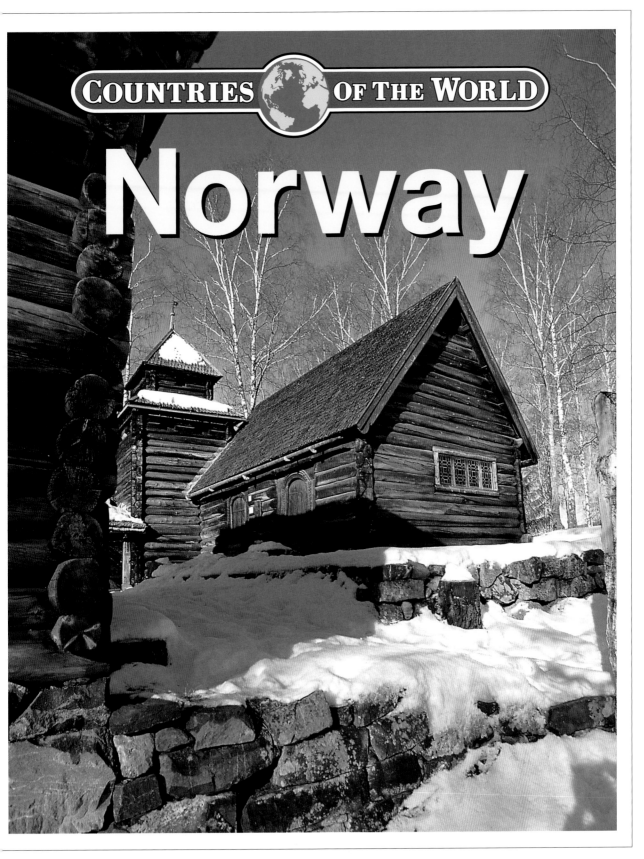

COUNTRIES OF THE WORLD

Norway

Gareth Stevens Publishing

A WORLD ALMANAC EDUCATION GROUP COMPANY

About the Author: Mike Hepso is a Norwegian-Canadian whose parents emigrated from Norway in 1957. Born in Canada, he spent part of his childhood in Norway and has returned for numerous visits. He has an Associate in Electronics Engineering Technology from Kwantlen University College and is currently living in British Columbia, Canada with his wife Laurie and their two sons, Lars and Jeremy.

PICTURE CREDITS
AFP: 60, 61 (top), 72, 75
Johan Berge: 23 (top)
Camera Press Limited: 77
Dave G. Houser/Houserstock, Inc: 1, 3 (top), 30, 32, 33 (bottom), 37
David Simson: 19
Ellen Barone/Houserstock, Inc: 20, 41, 67
Focus Team — Italy: 3 (center), 8, 23 (bottom), 51, 62, 68, 71, 89, 91
Getty Images/Hulton Archive: 11 (top), 12, 13, 14, 15 (top), 29 (right), 46, 52 (top), 58, 61 (bottom), 76, 81, 84, 85
Haga Library, Japan: cover, 3 (bottom), 21, 33 (top), 35, 38 (both), 42, 50, 63, 66
HBL Network Photo Agency: 2, 5, 6, 31, 34, 46, 43, 47 (top), 48, 55
Mike Hepso: 90
Hutchison Library: 16, 54, 65, 70 (both)
International Photobank: 4, 87
Jan Butchofsky/Houserstock, Inc: 18
Lonely Planet Images: 40 (both)
North Wind Picture Archives: 10, 69 (both)
Royal Canadian Mint: 83
Scanpix/Norway: 15 (bottom), 17, 24, 28, 29 (left), 39, 44, 45, 49, 53, 56, 57, 59 (both), 64, 73, 74, 78, 79, 80, 82
Sylvia Cordaiy Photo Library Limited: 7, 9, 22, 26
Topham Picturepoint: 11 (bottom), 25, 27 (both), 47 (bottom), 52 (bottom)

Digital Scanning by Superskill Graphics Pte Ltd

Written by
MIKE HEPSO

Edited by
LEONG WEN SHAN

Edited in the U.S. by
ALAN WACHTEL
PETER SCHMIDTKE

Designed by
GEOSLYN LIM

Picture research by
SUSAN JANE MANUEL

First published in North America in 2003 by
Gareth Stevens Publishing
A World Almanac Education Group Company
330 West Olive Street, Suite 100
Milwaukee, Wisconsin 53212 USA

Please visit our web site at
www.garethstevens.com
For a free color catalog describing
Gareth Stevens Publishing's list of high-quality
books and multimedia programs, call
1-800-542-2595 (USA) or 1-800-387-3178 (Canada)
Gareth Stevens Publishing's fax: (414) 332-3567.

© **TIMES MEDIA PRIVATE LIMITED 2003**
Originated and designed by
Times Editions
An imprint of Times Media Private Limited
A member of the Times Publishing Group
Times Centre, 1 New Industrial Road
Singapore 536196
http://www.timesone.com.sg/te

Library of Congress Cataloging-in-Publication Data
Hepso, Mike.
Norway/by Mike Hepso.
p. cm. — (Countries of the world)
Summary: An overview of Norway that includes information on geography, history, government, language, culture, and current issues.
Includes bibliographical references and index.
ISBN 0-8368-2362-1 (lib. bdg.)
1. Norway—Juvenile literature.
[1. Norway.] I. Title.
II. Countries of the world (Milwaukee, Wis.)
DL409.H47   2003
948.1—dc21   2002026855

Printed in Malaysia

1 2 3 4 5 6 7 8 9 07 06 05 04 03

Contents

5 AN OVERVIEW OF NORWAY

6 Geography
10 History
16 Government and the Economy
20 People and Lifestyle
28 Language and Literature
30 Arts
34 Leisure and Festivals
40 Food

43 A CLOSER LOOK AT NORWAY

44 Constitution Day
46 Dauntless Explorers
48 Fabulous Fjords
50 Fantastic Folklore
52 Henrik Ibsen: Father of Modern Drama
54 Oslo
56 Petroleum
58 Resistance during World War II
60 The Royal Family
62 The Sami
64 Saving Norway's Lakes and Oceans
66 Traditional Clothes
68 Valorous Vikings
70 Vigeland's Artistry
72 Women in Norway

75 RELATIONS WITH NORTH AMERICA

For More Information ...
86 Full-color map
88 Black-and-white reproducible map
90 Norway at a Glance
92 Glossary
94 Books, Videos, Web Sites
95 Index

AN OVERVIEW OF NORWAY

Located in northern Europe, the Kingdom of Norway is part of Scandinavia and is known for its mythic trolls, stunning fjords, and epic Viking past. The country is one of Europe's most mountainous places, and with 4.5 million inhabitants, it has the lowest population density in the whole of Europe. Norway also has one of the highest standards of living in the world. Its strong economy secures its population's material well-being, and its extensive social programs and welfare benefits ensure that every citizen receives certain services. As one of the founding members of the United Nations (U.N.), Norway has participated in humanitarian projects in developing nations and is committed to helping to resolve international conflicts.

Opposite: **Glaciers are part of Norway's unique landscape.**

Below: **Cabins line many placid fjords in Norway and attest to the Norwegians' fondness for nature.**

THE FLAG OF NORWAY

From 1397 to 1814, Norway was part of a union with Denmark, and as a result, Denmark's flag flew over Norway. In 1814, Norway left the union with Denmark and entered a union with Sweden. Because Sweden was the dominant power in the union, the Swedish flag flew over Norwegian skies until 1899. The Norwegian flag consists of a blue Scandinavian cross outlined in white on a red background. Designed by Frederik Meltzer in 1821 in a bid for independence, the Norwegian flag faced a seventy-eight-year struggle before it was officially hoisted on December 15, 1899.

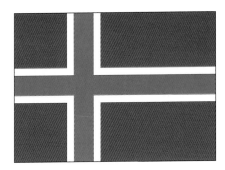

5

Geography

Norway's mainland covers an area of 118,834 square miles (307,860 square kilometers), with nearly fifty thousand islands lying off its coast. The country shares borders with Sweden, Finland, and Russia. Nearly a third of Norway lies north of the Arctic Circle, and its coasts border the Norwegian Sea, the North Atlantic Ocean, and the North Sea.

Mountains and Glaciers

Norway's coastline is 13,624 miles (21,925 kilometers) long. Its coasts are marked by many fjords, making the coastline very rugged. Aside from fjords, Norway also has several glaciers. The largest is Jostedalsbreen, which occupies 189 square miles (490 square km). Two-thirds of the terrain is mountainous, and only 3 percent of the land can be used for growing crops. At 8,100 feet (2,469 meters), the highest point in Norway is Galdhöpiggen.

THE GLÅMA

The 372-mile-(599-km-) long Glåma River is the country's longest river. The river serves as an important source of hydroelectric power and is also used to transport timber.

Below: Sogne Fjord is the longest and deepest fjord in Norway.

6

Geographical Regions

Traditionally, Norway has been divided into four geographical regions: Østlandet in the east, Trøndelag in the center, Vestlandet in the west, and Nord-Norge in the north. Mountain ranges separate these regions.

A land of broad valleys and rolling hills, Østlandet is the most densely populated area of Norway. Oslo, the nation's capital, is located in this region.

Trøndelag is similar in formation to Østlandet, with vast hills, wide valleys, and steep fjords. The plains around the city of Trøndheim are largely used for forestry and agriculture.

Vestlandet is characterized by fjords and snowy mountains that descend sharply to the sea. The largest city in this region is Bergen, which serves mainly as a commercial center.

Nord-Norge makes up a third of Norway and is sparsely populated. Most inhabitants of this region have settled on the coasts, where fishing is a major industry.

Recently, Sørlandet, in southern Norway, has been recognized as a distinct region. Previously part of Østlandet, Sørlandet is the smallest of all the regions. It occupies only 5 percent of Norway's mainland. Nonetheless, it produces as much as 10 percent of the country's hydroelectric power.

Above: **Trøndheim was the first capital of Norway. Previously called Nidaros, the city was founded in A.D. 997.**

SAVING NORWAY'S LAKES AND OCEANS

Air pollution and disease are now posing serious threats to the aquatic life in Norway.

(A Closer Look, page 64)

FABULOUS FJORDS

Numerous fjords dot Norway's landscape, enhancing the natural beauty of the country.

(A Closer Look, page 48)

Seasons and the Climate

Despite its northerly location, Norway has a pleasant climate. In winter, all parts of Norway typically have cold winter climates with snow. The western coast has a marine climate, with milder winters and cooler summers than the rest of the country. Annual rainfall along the western coast can be as much as 80 inches (203 centimeters). The temperate weather conditions along the coast are due to the North Atlantic Current of the Gulf Stream. The Gulf Stream brings in warm water that keeps the fjords and harbors virtually ice-free during winter.

Eastern Norway is sheltered from the coastal weather by mountains and has cold winters and warm summers. Annual rainfall in this area is less than 30 inches (76 cm). In Oslo, the temperature falls to 25° Fahrenheit (-4° Celsius) during winter and rises to 61° F (16° C) in summer.

From mid-May through July, the sun does not set completely in the part of the country that lies within the Arctic Circle. This northern area is called the "Land of the Midnight Sun." Here, the long summer days gradually transform into long winter nights. Consequently, from the end of November to mid-January, the northernmost parts of the country do not get any sunlight.

Above: **The warm current of the Gulf Stream keeps the country's fjords and harbors ice-free even during Norway's cold winters.**

LAND OF THE MIDNIGHT SUN

The Arctic Circle marks the southernmost latitude where constant daylight or night can be experienced. Twenty-four hours of daylight occur around June 21. The sun does not rise at all for a day or so around December 21.

Plants and Animals

More than a third of Norway's land area is covered by forests. In the southern coastal districts, forests are primarily deciduous, while forests of spruce, pine, and birch thrive in the eastern and northern districts. The Norway spruce and the Scotch pine are traditionally used as Christmas trees.

Norway is rich in wild berries, including blueberries, yellow cloudberries, and cranberries. Cloudberry plants rarely grow in the wild outside Scandinavia and Britain.

Arctic animals, such as reindeer, lemmings, and wolverines, roam all parts of Norway, as do elks and red deer. Salmon and trout overrun the nation's lakes and rivers. Large animals such as bears and wolves were a common sight, but their numbers have declined. In Norway, the cuckoo's call can frequently be heard from afar, even though this bird shies away from humans and is rarely spotted. Of the many varieties of birds found in Norway — ranging from Arctic terns to common cranes — some migrate as far south as Africa for winter.

NATIONAL FLOWER

Norway's national flower is the purple heather, a hardy plant that grows abundantly throughout the country.

Below: Herds of domesticated goats wander freely in the countryside. Animals in Norway are well-protected by the strict laws of the Norwegian Animal Welfare Act.

History

Arriving around twelve thousand years ago, hunters and fishermen are believed to be among the earliest inhabitants of Norway. From 3,000 B.C. to 2,500 B.C., more settlers moved into the area. These people farmed and raised livestock.

The Vikings, the Plague, and the Unions

Gradually, these early settlers were displaced by more aggressive, warlike people. The Vikings, Norway's most notorious ancestors, dominated the land from A.D. 800 to A.D. 1100. These bold warriors made their presence felt in the rest of Europe when they raided various settlements on the continent.

Through many battles in the later half of the ninth century, Viking chief Harald I Fairhair established his authority over the coastal districts of Norway and began uniting the country under his rule. Relations between subsequent Viking chiefs and Christian countries such as England and Normandy brought Christianity to Norway. A descendant of Harald Fairhair, Olaf II Haraldsson became king of Norway in the eleventh century. He increased royal power and continued Christianizing the country.

VALOROUS VIKINGS

The Vikings were among the early Scandinavians known as Norsemen. Odin, nicknamed "The Fury," was the chief god of the Norsemen. It was a great honor for a Norseman to die in battle because this meant his soul would be carried to Odin's court after death. *(A Closer Look, page 68)*

Below: **This print shows the Vikings during one of their devastating raids.**

A plague called the Black Death struck Norway from 1349 to 1350, killing about two-thirds of the population. This devastating epidemic led to the decline in the nation's wealth and power. In 1380, Norway and Denmark united under Danish King Olaf. By 1397, Norway, Sweden, and Denmark had formed the Kalmar Union. The Norwegian economy and culture declined during the union, and for the next four hundred years, Norway was ruled by Danish governors.

In 1814, Norway instituted its own constitution and became an independent nation. Its independence, however, was short-lived. Sweden attacked and defeated Norway within fourteen days. Charles XIII, the Swedish king, became Norway's ruler, though Norway maintained control of its internal affairs.

During the nineteenth century, Norway experienced massive growth in its economy, culture, and social systems. In addition, the country's population almost tripled between 1814 and 1900. Gradually, Norwegians gained a foothold in the struggle for complete independence, and parliamentary government replaced the king's cabinet in 1884. In 1905, the union with Sweden was dissolved, and Norway regained its independence.

Above: **The Black Death, or bubonic plague, struck most parts of Europe during the fourteenth century.**

Below: **King Oscar II, who ruled Sweden and Norway, renounced the Norwegian throne in 1905.**

The Norwegian Throne

After the end of the union with Sweden, Norway began to build on its newfound status as an independent state. Lacking a royal family of its own, the new Norwegian government elected the Danish prince Carl as king of Norway in 1905. As the first monarch in the present line of Norwegian royalty, Prince Carl took the name King Haakon VII.

The World Wars and the Great Depression

During the period of 1905 to 1914, Norway enjoyed economic growth. Social democracy also took huge steps forward; women could vote in local elections as early as 1907 and began taking part in national elections in 1913. By the time World War I began, Norway's merchant fleet was the fourth largest in the world.

At the outset of World War I in 1914, Norway declared itself neutral. Almost half of the Norwegian merchant fleet, however, was destroyed by the Germans because the ships carried cargo for the Allies, who fought against Germany.

THE ROYAL FAMILY

Prince Carl of Denmark was elected king by the Norwegian government in 1905.

(A Closer Look, page 60)

Below: **This picture shows a street in Oslo at the beginning of the twentieth century.**

The Great Depression that began in 1929 hit Norway hard, leaving one-third of the population unemployed. Even though the years between the two world wars were wrought with high unemployment and labor unrest, the country's industrial production increased by 75 percent.

At the beginning of World War II, in 1939, Norway again declared its neutrality. In 1940, however, Germany attacked Norway's major seaports. After two months of fighting, Norway surrendered, but the Nazi government, led by Norwegian National Socialist Party leader Vidkun Quisling, was met with strong resistance from the Norwegian public. Strikes and underground resistance movements against German industrial and military efforts in Norway began, but the Germans remained in Norway as an occupying force until 1945. By the time World War II ended, in 1945, some 10,262 Norwegians had been killed, while many cities in Norway had been destroyed.

After World War II, Norway began rebuilding its economy with the help of loans from the United States. The country especially worked to rebuild its industries. By 1950, Norway exceeded its prewar wealth.

Above: **The Norwegian merchant fleet helped Allied forces during wartime by carrying oil, supplies, and food to soldiers all over the world.**

RESISTANCE DURING WORLD WAR II

Many Norwegians proved their loyalty to their country during World War II by becoming active in the resistance movement aimed at stopping the German war machine.

(*A Closer Look, page 58*)

From Neutrality to Activism

Norway became a founding member of the United Nations in 1945, and Norwegian Minister of Foreign Affairs Trygve Lie became the U.N.'s first secretary-general. Realizing that it could not remain neutral in the event of war, Norway joined the North Atlantic Treaty Organization (NATO) in 1949.

Norway also participates in the Organization for Security and Cooperation in Europe (OSCE), which works on conflict prevention, post-crisis management, and arms control.

In 1952, the Nordic Council, which consists of Norway, Sweden, Finland, Denmark, and Iceland, was formed. This agreement allows citizens from each of the five countries to travel and work freely in any of the other four countries.

In 1994, Norway was invited to join the European Union (EU), but over half of the population voted against joining the union. Today, the Norwegian government is focusing on economic stability and social welfare. Thanks to the social welfare system, Norwegian citizens enjoy security through programs passed in accordance with the National Insurance Act, including pensions for the elderly and benefits for the disabled.

Below: **NATO's fiftieth anniversary was held in Washington, D.C. on April 23, 1999.**

Olaf II Haraldsson (c. 995–1030)

Also called Saint Olaf, Olaf II Haraldsson was the first king of all Norway. A descendant of the Norwegian ruler Harald I Fairhair, Olaf II was a Viking warrior. He ruled the country after returning to Norway from England. Olaf II died in battle in 1030, and the mystery surrounding his death — which is said to have involved miracles — along with his popularity, created a legend. His popularity spread, and shrines were constructed in his honor in England, Sweden, and even Rome, Italy. Olaf was canonized in 1164 and became Norway's patron saint.

Fridtjof Nansen (1861–1930)

Fridtjof Nansen

Fridtjof Nansen was an explorer, statesman, and humanitarian. He explored Greenland in 1882 and 1888, and explored the polar regions from 1893 to 1896, reaching further north than anyone else of his time. In *The First Crossing of Greenland* (1890), *Farthest North* (1897), and *The Norwegian North Polar Expedition* (1900–1906), Nansen wrote about his explorations. In 1905, Nansen advocated the separation of Sweden and Norway. He then served as Norway's minister to Britain from 1906 to 1908 and, in 1920, as a delegate to the Assembly of the League of Nations. In 1922, Nansen received the Nobel Peace Prize for his tireless work for the Red Cross during the famine in Russia. In 1931, the League of Nations honored him by creating the Nansen International Office for Refugees, which won the Nobel Peace Prize in 1938.

Gro Harlem Brundtland (1939–)

Gro Harlem Brundtland

Dr. Gro Harlem Brundtland was Norway's first female prime minister. A trained physician, she worked for nine years in the Ministry of Health and contributed greatly to children's health and disease prevention. Brundtland was appointed Minister of the Environment in 1974. At the age of forty-one, in 1981, she became the prime minister of Norway. Affectionately referred to as "Gro" by Norwegians, Brundtland served as prime minister for more than ten years. After a career in politics, she was appointed Director-General of the World Health Organization (WHO) in 1998.

Government and the Economy

Norway is a constitutional monarchy. The king is the hereditary head of state and plays more than just a ceremonial role in representing the people. The Council of State, which consists of an elected Prime Minister and other ministers appointed by the king, holds executive power within the government. The country is run according to its constitution, which was drafted in 1814. With the exception of a few minor amendments, the constitution has not been changed since then.

The Norwegian legislative body, which has 165 members, is called the *Storting* (STOOR-teeng). The Storting consists of the *Lagting* (LOG-teeng), or upper house, which makes up one-fourth of it, and the *Odelsting* (OO-dels-teeng), or lower house. For a bill to become a law, it must be voted on by the members of both the Odelsting and the Lagting. The monarch has veto power, which is the right to reject bills or courses of action that the Storting recommends. Since the union with Sweden ended in 1905, however, this power has never been used.

WOMEN IN NORWAY

In the 1990s, more than one-third of the representatives in the Storting were women.
(A Closer Look, page 72)

Below: The Storting building is located in Oslo, Norway's capital.

16

National elections are held every four years in Norway. Political parties nominate candidates in each of the nation's nineteen counties before each election. Based on the size of its population, each county elects a proportional number of representatives to the Storting. Eight representatives are elected by the whole country.

Since 1965, no single party has been successful in gaining a majority in the Storting. Consequently, Norway has been governed by minority governments, or governments made up of many parties, none of which holds the majority of seats. Today, Norway has twenty-four registered political parties, eight of which are represented in the Storting.

A chief justice heads the Supreme Court in Norway. The Ministry of Justice nominates judges for the various courts, and these judges are then appointed by the king. Impeachment cases, or cases in which accusations of misconduct are filed against public officials, are heard by the High Court of the Realm.

Above: **The king of Norway attends a session of the Storting in Oslo.**

THE LABOR PARTY

Until 1965, the Labor Party had a strong following. The party adopted a moderate form of socialism and was responsible for setting up many of the social programs in place today.

Industrial Resources

By the mid-1990s, Norway was one of the world's largest exporters of petroleum, second only to Saudi Arabia. This industry accounted for 46 percent of the country's total exports in 2000.

Norway has many river systems that lie on high plains. Power plants and dams that have been built along waterfalls, rivers, and melting glaciers provide electricity for the country. Norway is Europe's largest producer of hydroelectric energy (per capita) and has more than 850 hydroelectric power plants.

Agriculture, Forestry and Fishing

Farms in Norway are small and usually family-owned. In 2000, the domestic agricultural product made up barely 1 percent of the gross national product.

Productive forests occupy 22 percent of the land in Norway, mainly in the eastern and central parts of the country. Most forest land is owned by individuals. The forest industry is Norway's third-largest export industry.

Along the Norwegian coast, where about half of the fishermen fish as their sole occupation, fishing is an important yet shrinking part of the economy. Between 1960 and the mid-1990s, the number of fishermen decreased to fewer than 24,000.

PETROLEUM

Oil was discovered in the North Sea in the 1960s. Since then, the petroleum industry has become an important factor in the Norwegian economy.
(A Closer Look, page 56)

Exports and Imports

Norway's many exports include machinery, fish, metals, and metal products. Most of the country's petroleum exports go to nations in the EU. Norway's largest trading partners include Germany, Sweden, and the United Kingdom. Foreign imports to Norway include heavy machinery and equipment, as well as manufactured and consumer goods.

Working Life

About three quarters of Norwegians work in the service sector, while about one-sixth work in industries such as manufacturing, mining, and petroleum. About 6 percent of the population is employed in the construction sector. The Norwegian economy also has one of the highest percentages of women in its workforce. The age of retirement in Norway is sixty-seven, and while unemployment has remained around 3 percent, the Directorate of Labor continues to support job-seekers with relevant job training.

LABOR LAWS

Norwegian employees enjoy four weeks of paid leave each year. In addition, working hours cannot exceed forty hours a week or nine hours a day.

Below: **This timber mill is located in Telemark.**

People and Lifestyle

Scandinavians are known around the world for having blond hair and blue eyes. Although this is not true for all Norwegians, many do have blond hair, and approximately 60 to 70 percent of the population has blue eyes. With the exception of the Finnish-speaking people and the Sami, the population of Norway is homogeneous.

The Sami are a main minority group in Norway. As Norway's first inhabitants, the Sami arrived in the country more than ten thousand years ago, probably from Central Asia. Today, approximately forty thousand Sami live in Norway, mainly in the northern parts of the country. The Sami Parliament opened in 1989, thus giving the country's Sami population a voice in Norwegian politics.

Finns first started to migrate to Norway in the eighteenth century. Some Finns came to Norway to seek a better life in the fjords of Troms and Finnmark, while others came to escape from fighting with Sweden and the famine that struck Finland in the 1860s. Today, a large part of the population in Finnmark is Finnish-Norwegian.

The rate of population growth in Norway is less than 0.5 percent per year.

LIFE EXPECTANCY

In Norway, the life expectancy is seventy-six years for men and eighty-two years for women.

Left: **About 77 percent of the population lives in urban areas. Due to Norway's extensive social welfare system and high standard of living, the cities are free of slums.**

TRADITIONAL CLOTHES

Norwegians still wear the country's traditional clothing today, especially during special occasions such as weddings.
(*A Closer Look, page 66*)

Other Minority Groups

Apart from the Finnish-speaking population and the Sami, other significant minority groups that have made their homes in Norway include Ethiopians, Pakistanis, Iranians, Swedes, and Danes. These groups make up over 6 percent of the population.

During the 1960s, Norway welcomed migrant workers from Turkey, Pakistan, India, and Morocco, but a ban has been imposed since 1975. Nevertheless, Norway still accepts asylum seekers and refugees. The number of asylum seekers increased sharply in the 1980s, with most of them coming from Chile, Sri Lanka, Iran, Poland, the former Yugoslavia, and Somalia.

New citizens can receive free Norwegian language lessons that are taught in their native tongue. Immigrants are expected to learn to speak Norwegian and their school-aged children have to attend school.

Above: Sami families who have converted to Christianity enjoy festive foods during Easter, very much like the rest of the population of Norway.

THE SAMI

Traditionally, the Sami wear bright costumes and herd reindeer.

(A Closer Look, page 62)

Family Life

Norwegians have long enjoyed high standards of living. In 2001, the U.N. ranked Norway as having the highest standard of living in the world. This ranking was based on factors such as life expectancy, women's equality, and wealth distribution.

Families play an important role in Norwegian society and tend to be quite small, often with only two children. It is very common for both father and mother to work. Parental leave benefits are applicable to both parents if both are employed, while unemployed mothers can obtain a pregnancy grant from the government.

The welfare system, which includes the Ministry of Health and Social Affairs and the Ministry of Children and Family Affairs, is funded through taxes and businesses, such as the government-owned petroleum company. Recently, people have complained about the high taxes imposed to fund such programs.

Participation in Norway's national insurance program is mandatory. This program provides services such as retirement funds, unemployment benefits, cash benefits for single-parent families and disabled citizens, and job training.

Above: **Norwegian brides today may choose to wear a modern white bridal gown or the traditional Norwegian bridal costume. Traditional bridal costumes are usually worn with crowns decorated with spoon-shaped, silver bangles.**

In the City

Norwegian cities are clean and organized. Parks are abundant and easily accessible. Even in cities such as Oslo, wilderness areas are never far away, and Norwegians often take advantage of them. In Oslo, due to the increasing number of inhabitants, traffic and lack of parking pose problems. In 1990, a toll system for cars entering and leaving the city was implemented. Funds raised by this program go toward improving the nation's roads and public transportation.

Above: Old farms can still be found in the nation's countryside.

Rural Living

In many ways, rural life in Norway has changed very little in recent years. Norway is a mountainous country, and, historically, access to many areas was only possible by boat. This isolation has created many different dialects and distinctive communities throughout the country. For example, the designs of traditional costumes vary from place to place.

The Norwegian government has created programs for training rural youths. In addition, development funds are raised to improve conditions in rural areas so people will continue to live and work in these areas.

Below: The bustling city of Oslo is crowded with pedestrians and café patrons.

Education

"Education for all" is the basic concept of the education policy of Norway. All Norwegian children must attend school between the ages of six and sixteen. Made compulsory in 1827 by the Primary School Act, these ten years of education are split into three levels: lower primary, upper primary, and lower secondary. Sometimes, in less populated regions, schools are so small that different grades have to be combined into one classroom. It is also common to combine primary and lower secondary grades into one school.

The curriculum for students attending primary and lower secondary schools includes religion, Norwegian, and English. In addition, students may choose to study a third language, usually German or French.

Upper secondary school spans three years, after the three years of lower secondary school. It is free, optional, and prepares students for higher learning or work. Students can opt for either general or vocational studies.

LITERACY

Norway has one of the highest literacy rates in the world. This means that almost everyone above the age of fifteen can read and write.

STUDENTS WITH SPECIAL NEEDS

The Ministry of Education ensures that students with learning disabilities are guided by teachers who have the skills to educate them. Students' needs are assessed by experts who then select the kind of curricula that are best-suited to their abilities.

Left: Norwegian primary school children are not given grades for their schoolwork. Grading begins in secondary school.

Entrance to institutions of higher education is based on students' performance in upper secondary school. Except for a small number of private colleges, all higher education institutions are run by the government. Nonetheless, they remain independent of one another. The four universities in Norway are located in Oslo, Bergen, Trøndheim, and Tromsø. Founded in 1811, when Norway was still under Danish rule, the University of Oslo is the oldest in Norway. Four Nobel prize winners hail from the University of Oslo.

Above: **Sami children attend schools in which a specific curriculum addresses their cultural needs.**

The Sami Curriculum

In districts designated as Sami, a special curriculum has been developed to suit the needs of the Sami pupils. For students who are not Sami, the culture and traditions of the Sami community are taught within their curricula. The University of Tromsø has a center for Sami Studies.

Before and After School

Since 1999, all municipalities in Norway are required to provide daycare facilities before and after school hours for children in the first four grades. These facilities have to abide by regulations and rules imposed by the Ministry of Children and Family Affairs.

COLLEGES

Apart from its four universities, Norway has six private colleges, twenty-six state colleges, and two art colleges. This abundance of higher education facilities makes further learning accessible for all Norwegian students.

The Evangelical Lutheran Church

The Evangelical Lutheran Church was proclaimed the official church of Norway by the constitution of 1814. Norway's clergy is nominated by the king, and the church is supported by the state. About 86 percent of Norwegians are members of the Evangelical Lutheran Church. Most Lutherans are baptized as children, confirmed at the age of fourteen, and married in church, though few attend church regularly.

The nation's conversion to Christianity started with the Vikings toward the end of the tenth century. During their travels to other lands, including Normandy and England, some Vikings converted to Christianity. They then returned to Norway, bringing this new religion with them.

Religion is a standard part of the public school curriculum. Students learn the Bible through hymns, storytelling, and open discussions on beliefs and philosophies. The tenets of other religions are also taught to foster understanding and acceptance.

Other religious groups in Norway include Free Lutherans, Methodists, Baptists, Pentecostals, and Roman Catholics. A large Muslim community is present in the Oslo region.

Above: **This Lutheran church service in Finnmark is attended by Sami people.**

FREEDOM OF WORSHIP

Although Lutheranism is the official religion of Norway, members of other religions still enjoy complete freedom of worship.

FEMALE CLERGY

King Olav V appointed the nation's first female pastor in 1961. Norway's first female bishop is Rosemarie Kohn, who was appointed in 1993.

Ancient Norse Gods

The pagan gods of the Norsemen of northern Europe date back centuries. Some of the Norse gods include Odin, god of war and wisdom; Thor, god of thunder and storms; Frey, god of fertility and peace; Tyr, the bravest fighter among the gods; and Freya, Earth goddess and patron of pleasure.

Odin was the father of all the gods and a protector of heroes. During battles, Odin sent maidens, called Valkyries, to lead fallen Viking warriors to Valhalla. Valhalla was the great hall of Asgard, the realm of the Norse gods. Here, the souls of slain warriors enjoyed a never-ending feast with Odin.

Odin's son, Thor, was also very popular among the Vikings. Thor had control over the weather and carried a hammer, which he used to make thunder. Norsemen used to scatter bread and pour wine on their fields as offerings to Frey when sowing their crops since Frey was the god of fertility, and they believed making such offerings would yield good harvests.

Today, Norwegians do not practice the old pagan religion, but they do enjoy the myths of the Norse gods for their exciting stories and poetic language.

Below: **Freya (*right*) is the sister of Frey, and she is the goddess of love in Norse mythology. Odin (*left*) is the Norse god of wisdom and war.**

27

Language and Literature

Language

The present Norwegian language belongs to the north Germanic group of languages that began as a combination of dialects that were spoken in Scandinavia around the eleventh century. Due to their similar linguistic ancestry, Norwegians can understand and communicate with people who speak Swedish and Danish.

The two officially recognized forms of Norwegian are New Norwegian, or *Nynorsk* (NEE-nohrsk), and Dano-Norwegian, or *Bokmål* (BOOK-mohl), also known as "Book Language." Bokmål, which developed during the union with Denmark, is more commonly used in Norway; newspapers and books are often written in Bokmål. This form of Norwegian is similar to written Danish but is pronounced differently. Nynorsk, which was previously called *Landsmål* (LAWNDS-mohl), was created in the mid-nineteenth century by linguist Ivar Aasen and is a blend of the several dialects spoken throughout the country.

RUNES

Runes are an ancient method of writing that have been used since the third century in Scandinavia, Britain, and Northern Europe. Early forms of the runic alphabet had twenty-four letters. Runes were probably developed by the Goths, who were Germanic.

A NEW LANGUAGE

Although Bokmål is still the most popular form of the Norwegian language, many people in Norway want a language entirely separate from Danish. Recently, efforts have been made to combine Nynorsk and Bokmål into *Samnorsk* (SAWM-nohrsk), a new language that is unique to Norwegians.

Left: A group of girls check the latest posters at a movie theater. The posters are written in Norwegian. The Norwegian alphabet has three more letters — æ, ø, and å — than the English alphabet.

Left: **Knut Hamsun (1859–1952) (***right***), and Sigrid Undset (***left***) are two of Norway's Nobel Prize-winning authors.**

Saami Dialects

The Sami have their own dialects that are related to Finnish and Hungarian. Norwegian-speaking people do not understand these Sami dialects. The three main dialect groups are Central Saami, East Saami, and South Saami. Within these groups are subgroups that are peculiar to inhabitants of specific regions. More than half of the Sami population speak Saami dialects.

Literature

Bjørnstjerne Bjørnson (1832–1910) is one of Norway's most well-loved writers. He was awarded the Nobel Prize for Literature in 1903. One of his poems, "Ja, vi elsker dette landet," was set to music and later became the Norwegian national anthem.

Sigrid Undset (1882–1949) won the Nobel Prize in 1928 for her historical novel, *Kristin Lavransdatter*. Set in the fourteenth century, this international classic was made into a film in 1995.

The saga is a type of literature that chronicles Viking history. Sagas consist of historical stories that were written mostly in Old Norse or Icelandic and passed down from one generation to the next. Aside from historical accounts of Viking adventures and valuable insights into the various Norwegian Viking rulers, sagas also provide detailed descriptions of the Vikings' sea travels.

FANTASTIC FOLKLORE

Aside from its literary achievements, Norway also has a wealth of enchanting folk tales.
(A Closer Look, page 50)

HENRIK IBSEN: FATHER OF MODERN DRAMA

The most famous Norwegian writer is dramatist Henrik Ibsen (1828–1906). Known as "The Father of Modern Drama," his plays often dealt with issues that were unexplored in traditional theater. Ibsen wrote works that were realistic at a time when plays were generally lighthearted.
(A Closer Look, page 52)

Arts

Architecture

Due to Norway's abundant timber resources, wood plays an important part in the architectural design of Norwegian buildings. Homes in Norway are often finished with pine walls and hardwood floors.

In the past, wood, which was easier to work with, was used to build common homes, while stone was used only by the wealthy. The well-to-do ended up in drafty stone buildings, while the lower classes lived in the natural warmth of wooden houses.

In the far northern part of the country, due to the lack of available wood and stone, the Sami found ways of using turf to build their homes. Turf provided excellent insulation during the long, cold winters.

Most of Norway's older churches are made of stone, while others, such as the famous stave churches, are made of wood.

VIGELAND'S ARTISTRY

Gustav Vigeland is probably Norway's best known sculptor. Vigeland Park in Oslo has more than two hundred of his statues. His earlier works are now displayed in the Vigeland Museum in Oslo. *(A Closer Look, page 70)*

Below: The Nidaros Cathedral features gothic arches. In 1897, Norwegian sculptor Gustav Vigeland restored certain parts of the cathedral.

Stave Churches

When the Vikings converted to Christianity about a thousand years ago, wooden churches, called stave churches, were built throughout the country. The roofs of stave churches are high and their interior walls are often painted with elaborate designs that include traditional rose paintings. Viking-age dragon heads and carvings on door frames, outer walls, and the wooden support posts called staves often decorate these churches. In 1979, the Urnes Stave Church was listed as a World Heritage site by the United Nations Educational, Scientific, and Cultural Organization (UNESCO) for its representative architectural design.

Folk Art, Orchestras, and Film

Cities such as Oslo, Bergen, Trøndheim, and Stavanger are important centers for the arts. Oslo's National Gallery is the country's largest art museum. The Norwegian Folk Museum, also in Oslo, displays artifacts of regional and national folk culture. Norway's chief orchestra is the Oslo Philharmonic, while other orchestras can be found in Bergen and Trøndheim. The Norwegian Film Institute, which markets and distributes Norwegian and foreign films, is located in Oslo. An international film festival is held in Haugesund each year.

Painters

Norway has produced a number of prominent painters. One of the country's most well-known painters is Edvard Munch. Born in Løten in 1863, Munch expressed intense emotions through his works, which influenced many painters that came after him. His most famous work, *The Scream*, was painted in 1893. Munch donated all his works to the city of Oslo before his death in 1944, and the Munch Museum was established in Oslo in 1963.

Other Norwegian painters, such as Alf Rolfsen (1895–1979) and Axel Revold (1887–1962), have gained international recognition for their mural artwork.

Delicate Rosemaling

Rosemaling (ROO-seh-mohling) is a traditional Norwegian form of painting. Meaning "rose painting," rosemaling features painted flowers arranged in decorative curls and twists. Inspired by a wide variety of painting styles, rosemaling was popular in urban, upper-middle class homes in the 1600s. Today, rosemaling graces common items, such as bowls and plates. The patterns are usually passed from generation to generation, although contemporary styles are also created.

OSLO

Oslo is the artistic capital of Norway, where all the major museums are located. This city was once called Kristiana when Norway was united with Sweden.

(*A Closer Look, page 54*)

A Rich Musical Legacy

Ole Bornemann Bull (1810–1880) was Norway's first virtuoso violinist. Born in 1810, he was hailed throughout Europe as the "Nordic Paganini." Bull performed throughout Europe, promoting Norwegian music to a wider audience.

Edvard Grieg (1843–1870) is probably Norway's best-known composer. Taught by his mother to play the piano, Grieg entered the Leipzig Conservatory in 1858 with the recommendation of Norwegian violin virtuoso Ole Bull. While his orchestral works were influenced by Norwegian folk songs and dances, some of his most popular pieces, such as *Opus 23* and the *Holberg Suite, Opus 40*, were composed for Ibsen's play, *Peer Gynt* (1867).

The Hardanger fiddle is a native Norwegian instrument that looks like an ordinary violin but has a unique sound because of the additional set of strings beneath the ones that are played. This uniquely Norwegian instrument is used in folk music.

Joik (YOYK) is a type of folk music that is sung by the Sami. A type of yodeling that mimics wolves and reindeers, joik songs usually tell the audience a story from a highly personal angle.

Above: Edvard Grieg is still recognized as one of Norway's most well-known composers.

Below: A musician displays his highly ornamented Hardanger fiddle (*right*) at the Norwegian Folk Museum in Oslo.

Leisure and Festivals

The Great Outdoors

Norwegians love the wilderness, which is often only a short ride away from the city. Even downtown Oslo is only a twenty-minute drive from the nearest forest. The Norwegian government has passed a law known as *Allemannsretten* (AWL-leh-mawns-reht-ten), or "Every Man's Right," which allows people to go wherever they desire. Therefore, "Keep Out" signs are rare in Norway.

Many families in Norway own cabins that are inaccessible by car, so they usually hike to reach them. These cabins are rustic, and they often have no electricity. Instead, lanterns and candles provide lighting in the evenings. People in Norway cherish nature, and they think living in a setting without modern conveniences is a refreshing break from everyday life.

Winter Activities

On weekends in winter, the snowy hills teem with cross-country skiers. During Easter vacation, many Norwegians head off to the

DAUNTLESS EXPLORERS

The adventurous spirit of the Norwegians is highly visible in the number of explorers that hailed from the country, especially in the twentieth century.
(A Closer Look, page 46)

Below: **Many Norwegian families enjoy boating.**

mountains. Some ski to remote cabins, while others take day trips to snow-covered hills. For lunch, they cook food over an open fire built on the snow.

Above: **Norwegian children play a game of tug-of-war as adults look on.**

While still at school, children go on nature trails, where they are sometimes taught how to snow camp. Such trips provide time with friends, and the skills learned on these trips may prove to be lifesaving at times when the environment is hostile.

Summer Pursuits

Norwegians enjoy the outdoors in summer as well. Instead of skiing, they often swim or fish. Another popular summer activity is hiking to the mountains; hikers often search for wild berries in the mountains. Norway's forests and hills are rich with berries that can be used to make delicious traditional jams and desserts. Due to the nation's numerous fjords, lakes, and rivers, the Norwegian landscape attracts fishing enthusiasts and sailors.

Socializing with Friends

When Norwegians are not enjoying the great outdoors, they are often visiting friends. Eating out is expensive, and most Norwegians prefer to spend time with friends in their homes.

Above: **This skier is one of many fans of skiing in Norway.**

Exhilarating Ski Sports

Considered the birthplace of skiing, Scandinavia is a winter wonderland. The need to get around in the snow gave rise to skiing, and the oldest known record of skiing is a rock carving at Rødøy of two people on skis that dates back to 2000 B.C.

Today, Norwegians love to ski, and they are particularly fond of cross-country skiing. Competitive cross-country skiers are often accompanied by a medical team to ensure that training at high altitudes and low temperatures does not endanger them. Alpine skiing, or downhill skiing, is also popular, but this sport does not have as many enthusiasts as cross-country skiing.

Ski jumping is a favorite sport among Norwegian adventurers. Charging down a long, narrow slope built at the top of a hill or mountain, ski jumpers jump off the snowy slope by straightening their bodies and leaning forward. The aim is to jump as far as possible and to land smoothly. In 1862, Norway held the world's first ski jumping contest in Trysil. One of the most terrifying ski jumps in the world, the Holmenkollen Ski Jump, was built in 1892. This ski jump was rebuilt for the 1952 Winter Olympics in Oslo. The annual Holmenkollen Ski Festival is the most eagerly anticipated sports event in Norway.

SPEED SKATING

Another popular winter sport at which Norwegians excel is speed skating. Norwegian speed skater Johann Olav Koss won three gold medals at the 1994 Winter Olympic Games, held in Lillehammer, Norway.

Summer Sports

In summer, the most popular sport in Norway is soccer. Known as *fotball* (FOOT-bawl), the game is played by children in parks and open spaces throughout the country. The Norwegian Football Association was formed in 1902, and the country's men's national soccer team qualified for the World Cup in 1938, 1994, and 1998. Their greatest success, however, was at the 1936 Olympic Games, where they won a bronze medal.

The country's women's national soccer team has excelled in international competitions. The team won a gold medal at the 2000 Olympic Games in Sydney, Australia, a bronze medal at the 1996 Olympic Games in Atlanta, a silver medal in the 1991 World Cup tournament, and a gold medal in the 1995 World Cup tournament.

Orienteering, a relatively new sport in Norway, is drawing participants from around the world. Practiced throughout the year, participants are placed in unfamiliar surroundings. Using maps, compasses, and their orienteering knowledge, they must navigate through checkpoints and finally to the finish point.

Below: A summer regatta begins at the harbor in Tromsø.

Midsummer's Eve

Sankthansaften (SAWNKT-hawns-awf-tehn), or Midsummer's Eve, is held on June 23 — shortly after the longest day of the year. Midsummer's Eve celebrations began during the time following the Christianization of the Vikings. In the past, people believed that after midnight on Midsummer's Eve, witches and evil spirits roamed the countryside. To protect themselves, people lit bonfires. This tradition lives on today, although the bonfires are no longer lit to ward off evil spirits. Instead, they are cozy meeting places for friends and family to welcome the summer season together.

Left: **Lighting bonfires to mark Midsummer's Eve festivities is one of the oldest celebrations in northern Europe.**

Easter Week

Easter is the time that Christians remember the death and resurrection of Jesus Christ and give thanks for the sacrifices he made. Norwegians who choose to attend church do so on Easter Sunday or the evening before.

Throughout Norway, the entire Easter week — from Palm Sunday to Easter Monday — is a time of recreation and holiday. Working adults and school children get a week of vacation, during which many Norwegians head for the hills to hike or cross-country ski. Some make day trips, others stay at cabins, and the more adventurous snow camp.

EASTER CRIMES

Recently, following an "Easter crime" has become an increasingly popular activity during Easter in Norway. These thrillers are featured on television programs and radio shows. Clues are revealed on a daily basis, and people try to figure out "who did it." Reading crime novels is an alternative to indulging in the "Easter crime" trend.

Left: **Midsummer's Eve in Norway is incomplete without traditional clothing and dance.**

Left: **A young girl looks at her presents that are laid beneath the Christmas tree.**

CONSTITUTION DAY

On May 17, Norwegians celebrate the signing of the Norwegian Constitution of 1814. An important part of this celebration is a children's parade.
(A Closer Look, page 44)

Christmas

Jul (YOOL), or Christmas, celebrates the birth of Jesus Christ. At home, Norwegians decorate windows with wreaths and Advent stars. The Christmas tree, usually a pine or spruce, is put up on December 23 or on Christmas Eve morning. Aside from common decorations such as tinsel, small Norwegian flags are sometimes strung together and laced over the tree. Christmas gifts are placed beneath the tree.

Ringe julen (REEN-geh YOOL-ehn), or ringing in Christmas, is a popular tradition in Norway. At five o'clock on Christmas Eve, the ringing of church bells can be heard throughout the streets, signifying the start of Christmas. Norwegians have a tradition of celebrating Christmas on December 24 instead of on Christmas day. After a traditional Christmas Eve dinner, gifts are presented, and friends and families gather round to open them. After this, they may attend a church service.

THE LUCKY SINGLE ALMOND

Christmas dinner includes *julegrøt* (YOOL-eh-groht), or rice pudding containing a single almond. The traditional belief is that whoever gets the almond will have a year filled with good luck.

Food

Norwegians typically eat four times a day. They are among the world's largest consumers of fish, milk, and cheese, but they eat little red meat. The abundant berries that grow throughout the land are a favorite filling for many desserts.

Breakfast, or *frokost* (FROOK-oost), is an important meal for Norwegians since they usually eat small lunches. Breakfast may include porridge or other cereals and open-faced sandwiches topped with jam, cheese, cold meat, marinated herring, or smoked fish. Lunch, or *lunsj* (LOON-sh), is usually little more than a large snack. Common lunches include open-faced sandwiches made with cold meats, fish, or cheese. Some Norwegians favor a snack in between breakfast and lunch, called *formiddagsmat* (fawh-MIH-dawgs-mawt).

Middag (MIH-dawg), or dinner, is usually the only hot meal of the day and is eaten in the early evening. It can consist of soup, meat cakes or fish balls, potatoes, vegetables, and a dessert. A later evening meal called *kveldsmat* (keh-VELL-dis-mawt) may include sandwiches with tea or coffee.

Above: Along the coast of Norway, cod is cleaned and hung out to dry on wooden posts. In the past, fish were dried in this manner to stop them from spoiling quickly. While the dried cod can be eaten as it is, it can also be boiled and softened, and then served with potatoes.

BARTERING BUTTER

Back in the days when Norwegians bartered, or traded goods instead of buying them with money, butter was the most valuable trading item. Butter was molded into pyramidal sculptures and used as decoration at weddings. Original wooden butter molds can be seen in Norwegian museums today.

Left: A hot meal consisting of bread, seafood, and soup is served for dinner.

Left: Fresh seafood is widely available in Norwegian markets and makes up a substantial part of the Norwegian diet.

Norwegians love bread and usually use it to make open-faced sandwiches. Although there are nearly countless toppings available for these sandwiches, the most popular are brown goat cheese, liver pâte, salted herring, cold meats, and an assortment of sweet spreads that include chocolate and nut flavors. Many kinds of cream cheese spreads containing everything from shrimp to vegetables are also available. *Flatbrød* (FLAWT-brohd) is a crispy, wafer-thin bread that is commonly eaten with foods such as stews.

Other popular Norwegian foods are *gomme* (GOO-meh), a sweet milk dish that is eaten with waffles, and *rømmegrøt* (ROHM-meh-groht), or sour cream porridge that is often served at weddings.

Beverages

Norwegians love to drink coffee and fine teas throughout the day. Milk and soft drinks are also popular. Many Norwegians enjoy drinking beer, which is sometimes served with a strong, colorless liquor called aquavit. Aquavit, which is made from distilled potatoes, is often flavored with caraway seeds. Aquavit and beer are enjoyed with many salted and smoked dishes.

ACROSS THE LINE

Line aquavit, or *linje akevitt* (LIN-yeh AWKE-vit), is aquavit that is placed on a ship and transported across the equator, or "the line." Shipments of aquavit that make the round-trip across the equator are believed to be of better quality. The transporting ship's name is written on the back of the bottles.

A CLOSER LOOK AT NORWAY

As an affluent country with a booming economy and a highly evolved social welfare system, many people look to Norway as an excellent example of a developed nation. Behind this modern kingdom is a proud line of fearsome warriors, loyal citizens, and adventurous explorers. Norwegians, from the explorers to the resistance force during World War II, have shown themselves to be dauntless in the face of difficult challenges and unfavorable odds. The notorious exploits of the Vikings in centuries past are equally matched by the artistic achievements of Norway's playwrights, sculptors, and musicians.

Opposite: **Two Sami children and their grandmother wear colorful, traditional outfits.**

The discovery of Norway's crude oil resources in the 1960s has contributed significantly to the country's wealth, enabling the Norwegian government to address the many needs of the nation. Adults and children alike benefit from the nation's insurance program, while minority groups, such as the Sami, engage in a constant dialogue with the government in order to reduce inequalities. Women in Norway have many opportunities to fulfill multiple roles and demands. In addition, the land itself, with cities such as Oslo, provides an enchanting backdrop for the bustling nation.

Above: **The St. Olaf's Festival is celebrated annually, in memory of Norway's patron saint.**

Constitution Day

The Historical Significance of May 17

Following the defeat of Danish troops at the hands of the Swedish, Denmark had to hand over Norway to Sweden. Anxious to regain control of Norway, the Danish governor of Norway, Prince Christian Frederik, stirred patriotic feelings in the Norwegians by urging them to write their own constitution. A group of elected politicians, tradesmen, and farmers formed a National Assembly and met at Eidsvoll Verk in April 1814 to draft a new constitution and select a Norwegian king. On May 17, 1814, they emerged with a newly signed constitution and elected Prince Christian Frederik as their new king. Sweden rejected this move toward independence and sent troops into Norway. King Christian Frederik was forced to give up his throne, and the Swedish king became king of Norway and took control of Norway's foreign affairs. Sweden, however, was willing to compromise by allowing Norway to live by its new constitution.

May 17, Norway's Constitution Day, is called *Syttende Mai* (SIH-tehn-deh MEYE-ee). On this day, the nation celebrates the beginning of Norway's independence.

WORLD WAR II

When German troops occupied Norway during World War II, May 17 celebrations were banned. After the Germans left Norway in 1945, the tradition was revived.

Below: Members of different communities in Norway gathered in Eidsvoll Verk to draft their country's constitution in 1814.

The Nation Stops to Celebrate

For Norwegian children, May 17 is a day filled with games, food, and parades. For adults, it is an important date in history and an opportunity to show pride in their nation. Throughout the day, bands play the national anthem, and Norwegians wear their beautifully embroidered *bunader* (BOO-nad-der) to the street parades.

The actual events of the day vary from town to town, but the festivities usually begin with a flag-raising ceremony at a local school, church, or government building. Afterward, a children's parade starts, with the children waving their Norwegian flags to the cheering crowd of onlookers.

After the children's parade, each community starts its own celebrations, which may include speeches, games, contests, food, and concerts. It is common for several parties to combine into one large celebration at the center of a town or city.

On the afternoon of May 17, a citizens parade begins. In the past, only adults took part, but children now participate as well. Girl scouts, soccer teams, and religious groups are all represented in the parade.

Above: **Children dress in colorful bunader and wave Norwegian flags in front of the Royal Palace in Oslo on May 17.**

RUSS

Students who have just completed twelve years of school are perhaps the most colorful group in the May 17 parades. Easily recognizable in bright overalls that represent their schools, these teenagers, also called "russ," always have a fun time making jokes and performing antics.

45

Dauntless Explorers

Beginning with the Vikings, Norway has been a nation of explorers. Norwegian exploration continued into the twentieth century when two adventurers pushed the frontiers of the sea.

Roald Amundsen (1872–1928)

In 1903, Norwegian Roald Amundsen and a crew of six left on a journey to become the first to sail through the Northwest Passage, a route north of Alaska that joins the Pacific and Atlantic oceans. His 47-ton (43-tonne) ship, called the *Gjöa*, was stuck in ice for two years, but the westward flow of the ice eventually moved the *Gjöa*, helping its crew reach Yukon, Canada, in 1905.

Amundsen continued his explorations. On October 19, 1911, he set out with four other explorers on sleds pulled by sled dogs to reach the South Pole. They accomplished the feat in just over two months. Amundsen and his team stayed at the South Pole for three days to record scientific data before returning to their base camp on January 25, 1912.

In 1926, Amundsen, together with American explorer Lincoln Ellsworth and Italian engineer Umberto Nobile, became the first person to fly over the North Pole.

TRYING TO SAVE A FRIEND

In 1928, Roald Amundsen lost his life in a plane crash when he attempted to rescue his friend Umberto Nobile, whose dirigible had crashed at the island of Svalbard in Norway.

Left: Roald Amundsen (*right*) poses for a photograph before one of his flights.

46

Thor Heyerdahl (1914–2002)

Thor Heyerdahl wanted to prove his theory that people from ancient civilizations could have traveled across the oceans long before modern boats had been developed. He constructed a balsa-wood raft in the ancient Peruvian style and set out on a voyage to test his theory. In 1947, Heyerdahl, along with a small crew, successfully sailed the raft, named *Kon-Tiki*, from Peru to Polynesia.

In 1969, aboard the *Ra*, a vessel designed in the style of an Egyptian reed boat, Heyerdahl sailed from Morocco to the waters near Central America. He believed this voyage proved that Egyptian civilization might have influenced the pre-Columbian cultures of the Western Hemisphere.

Thor Heyerdahl led other expeditions that included sea journeys to the Maldive Islands, Easter Island, and Pakistan. During his expeditions, Heyerdahl devoted much of his study to the pollution in the oceans, and he wrote passionately on the subject.

Above: **The original *Kon-Tiki* is now on display at the Kon-Tiki Museum in Oslo.**

Below: **Heyerdahl's film about the *Kon-Tiki* won the Academy Award for Best Documentary in 1951.**

Fabulous Fjords

Norway is known for its magnificent fjords, many of which stretch deep into the mainland. These fjords, which form natural harbors, make Norway's coastline one of the longest in the world in relation to its land mass. The warm currents of the Gulf Stream keep the natural harbors free of ice during winter, even in the parts of Norway that lie in the Arctic Circle.

Fjords are narrow inlets from the sea that are flanked by steep walls that continue far below the water's surface. Fjords were originally rivers that ran westward toward the sea. During the Great Ice Age, glaciation created the U-shaped bottoms that fjords now have. As the glaciers melted and the oceans rose, the bottoms of the valleys filled with water, forming fjords.

The Fjords in Norway's History

Norway's fjord-pocketed coast has had a profound impact on the country's history. Because of this rough terrain, there was not enough land to grow crops, forcing the Vikings to go on journeys to find better agricultural land. In addition, numerous natural harbors created by the fjords ensured that good water access was never far away.

Left: **If the water was drained from the fjords, all that would remain are U-shaped bottoms with steep, mountainous walls.**

48

Famous Fjords

The longest and deepest fjord in Norway is Sogne Fjord. It is 127 miles (204 km) long and reaches a maximum depth of 4,265 feet (1,300 m). Touted as the "King of Fjords," Sogne Fjord is the deepest and longest fjord in the world. Some of the waterfalls in Sogne Fjord are used to generate hydroelectricity. The mouth of the Sogne Fjord is north of the city of Bergen.

Another of Norway's most scenic fjords is located in the Hardanger mountains, or Hardangervidda, in southern Norway. Commonly referred to as the "Queen of Fjords," the Hardanger fjord is the second largest fjord in Norway, with a length of 111 miles (179 km). Numerous fjords branch off this main fjord. In addition, Hardanger Fjord has fruit orchards and waterfalls that cascade down the steep mountain faces, making the fjord a popular destination spot for tourists.

Above: **The longest fjord in the world, Sogne Fjord is a scenic location that attracts Norwegians and tourists alike.**

Fantastic Folklore

Norwegian folklore is rich with stories of strange and enchanted creatures. In the past, people lived in small communities, and knowledge was restricted to the rural areas they inhabited. Folktales served a basic need for explaining the unknown. Even today, folktales remain an important part of Norwegian culture.

Enchanted Creatures

Probably the most famous creature in Norwegian folklore is the troll. Throughout the years, several versions of this creature have emerged. Early on, trolls were thought of as gigantic, monstrous, magical, and always hostile toward humans. They lived in huge castles and prowled at night. When exposed to sunlight, they would turn to stone and burst into flames.

Later, trolls were believed to be the same size as humans or slightly smaller. They were believed to live in the mountains and sometimes to kidnap maidens. They could prophesy and transform themselves into other things. In the past, many people believed mountains were actually trolls that transformed themselves. In modern folktales, trolls often live under a bridge and demand payment from people wishing to cross the bridge.

Left: **Troll figurines are displayed on the streets of Norway.**

One type of troll is the *nøkken* (NOK-kehn), a water spirit, that resides under waterfalls. The nøkken is an accomplished fiddler and can even teach people how to play the instrument.

One female troll in Norwegian folklore is the *hulder* (HOOL-der). The hulder, or wood nymph, is an ugly troll with a long, cow-like tail that sticks out from under her skirt. Although many contrasting versions of her story exist, they all agree that she can magically transform herself to become stunningly beautiful and that she tries to seduce unmarried young men with her beauty. The hulder's tail drops off when a man marries her in a church.

Another type of troll, the *nisse* (NIHS-seh) is a short, humanlike creature that is believed to live in barns. The nisse is known to wear a red cap and have a long beard. Legend has it that if the owners of the barn are good to the nisse, it looks after the livestock inside the barn in return. Similar to Santa Clause, the nisse is traditionally believed by some to help parents deliver presents to their children. Some Norwegian farmers today continue to place a gift or a bowl of porridge out in the barn on Christmas Eve for the nisse.

Henrik Ibsen: Father of Modern Drama

Referred to as "the father of modern drama," Henrik Ibsen was a playwright who blazed new trails in the world of theater. He is considered an innovator because he incorporated modern issues in his plays and focused more on character development rather than on plot.

Born in 1828, Ibsen lived in a small lumber town called Skien in southern Norway. Ibsen's home life took a turn for the worse when his father went bankrupt in 1836, and this strain pulled the family apart. When he turned fifteen, Ibsen moved to Grimstad. Wanting to study medicine, young Ibsen worked as an apothecary's apprentice while studying for his university entrance exams. During this time, he wrote a play called *Catiline* (1850). Although the play was not highly acclaimed, Ibsen was not deterred. After failing courses in mathematics and Greek, he decided against studying the sciences and turned to theater.

Ibsen worked in Kristiana (present-day Oslo) and Bergen. From this experience, he acquired a sharp eye for theatrical technique and went on to devote his entire life to theater.

Above: At the age of twenty-three, after a short stint in Kristiana, Ibsen became a playwright for a new theater in Bergen. This was good training for Ibsen, who wrote a new play every year.

Left: These actors are performing in a 1996 production of Ibsen's play *Ghosts* (1881).

Ibsen's Later Career

Between 1864 and 1891, Ibsen lived and worked in Munich, Rome, and Dresden. Although he received an annual pension granted by the Norwegian state, Ibsen felt the culture of Norway, at the time, was too narrow-minded. As a result, he did not return home until 1891 at the age of sixty-three.

Ghosts (1881), *The Master Builder* (1892), *A Doll's House* (1879), and *Peer Gynt* (1867) are some of Ibsen's most famous plays. Although his plays were sometimes shocking to the audiences of his day, Ibsen's critics praised him for dramatization of characters that were realistic and issues that were familiar.

Ibsen collaborated with Norwegian composer Edvard Grieg. Grieg wrote the music for Ibsen's *Peer Gynt*, which became one of the playwright's best-known works. Some of Ibsen's plays also incorporated Norwegian folklore, as was the case with *Peer Gynt*, in which trolls play an important role.

Above: Ibsen's *A Doll's House* explores the role of women in the family during the late nineteenth century. This play is still performed today.

Oslo

An Ancient City

The name "Oslo" comes from Old Norse and means "the fields of the gods." The city was founded by King Harald Hardraade around 1050. During the union with Denmark, Norway's politics were controlled by the Danes in Copenhagen, and Oslo declined in importance. In 1624, a fire ravaged much of the city, but it was rebuilt, mainly of stone, by King Christian IV of Denmark-Norway and renamed Christiania.

In 1814, when Norway and Sweden united, the city's name was changed to "Kristiana," the Swedish spelling for "Christiana." When the union was dissolved in 1905, Kristiana was again declared the capital of Norway. In 1925, its name was changed back to Oslo.

Below: Oslo does not have any skyscrapers, although the city has several modern glass and steel buildings. Many stone buildings that date back to the seventeenth century can still be seen, but because of the fire of 1624, few structures built before that year remain.

A Modern Hub

The commercial and economic center of the nation, present-day Oslo offers all the conveniences of a major city. Although it has a population of more than 500,000 inhabitants, the surrounding mountains and lakes give the urban area the added advantage of having nature at its doorstep.

The city is located at the northern end of the Oslo Fjord and rests inside a belt of pine-clad hills that has many beautiful lakes and marshes. This surrounding area is called Oslomarka, which means "Oslo Field," and is dedicated to outdoor life. The area has hiking and skiing trails, a ski jump, and picnic areas. In the waters of Oslo Fjord, windsurfers, sailboats, and canoes can be spotted alongside fishing boats and barges.

Oslo is the country's center of trade, banking, shipping, and industry. Oslo Harbor is the largest and busiest port in Norway, and electronics, shipbuilding, and the manufacture of consumer goods are among the city's important industries.

Completed in 1848, the Royal Palace is located on a hill in central Oslo. Renovated over the years, the palace has a ballroom with a 35 foot- (10.7 m-) high ceiling. In Oslo, historical museums, such as the Folk Museum, the Viking Ship Museum, and the Maritime Museum, allow for visual insight into Norway's past. The National Gallery, the Munch Museum, and Vigeland Park are also located in Oslo.

Above: **The Akershus Festning was built by King Haakon V in the fourteenth century to fend off possible attacks from Sweden.**

Petroleum

The petroleum industry in Norway only took off recently but has become an important part of the Norwegian economy. Today, the nation is one of the largest oil exporters in the world, second only to Saudi Arabia. All of Norway's major oil discoveries have been offshore, and the oil is extracted at offshore platforms.

Discovering Oil

Oil exploration began in 1966, but the first well drilled was not successful. Three years later, on December 23, 1969, workers on a drilling rig smelled oil. This breakthrough led to further oil discoveries, and, by the mid-1970s, a gas pipeline had been laid across the North Sea to Teesside, England. Production became so great that Norway started exporting oil to Germany and Scotland.

By the mid-1990s, Norway had become the world's second largest exporter of oil, with about half the country's export earnings and one-tenth of its government revenues coming from oil and gas. High rates of oil production can be sustained at least until 2020, and the country's natural gas reserves are currently estimated at 44 trillion cubic feet (1.2 trillion cubic m).

Left: In 2001, Norwegians drove their cars more than ever, and sales of gasoline increased by almost 4 percent.

The Troll Field

One of the largest offshore gas fields ever found, the Troll field is located west of Bergen. By the mid-1990s, more than 25 percent of Norway's huge offshore operations investment had gone into the Troll field, making it one of the largest energy projects in the world. When it was towed into place in 1995, the Troll A platform was the tallest concrete structure that had ever been moved. The Troll A production platform reaches a height of nearly 1,550 feet (472 m) and is 564 feet (172 m) long. The platform is expected to be productive for at least fifty years. The gas production of the Troll field makes Norway the leading supplier of natural gas to the European continent.

The Environment

In Norway, there is little need for natural gas since most people use electricity that is produced by the nation's hydroelectric dams. Thus, the population does not burn much fossil fuel, which harms the environment.

Above: **The Troll field (*above*) is one of the many oil fields in Norway. Although the early discoveries of oil were made by foreign companies, Norwegian companies, such as Statoil, Saga, and a third company that was established by Norsk Hydro, were soon established after the discovery of oil in Norway.**

Resistance during World War II

When World War II began in 1939, Norway declared its neutrality. On April 9, 1940, however, the German army invaded Norway. This move marked the end of Norway's neutrality and the beginning of a resistance movement against the Germans.

Upon Invasion

Soon after the German invasion, King Haakon VII, the crown prince, and all the members of the Norwegian government went into hiding to avoid being captured by the Nazis after refusing to submit to Germany's demands. Their refusal spurred resistance among military groups and civilians.

Sleds of Gold

As the Germans invaded Norway, Norwegians sought to hide their gold bullion for fear that the gold would be used to fund the German war effort. The resistance movement aimed to move the bullion to a harbor in Molde, where it would then be shipped to safety. In addition to trucks, trains, and ferries, children on sleds were employed to move the gold. With gold bullion hidden in snowmen, children on their way to the harbor sledded past German soldiers.

COLLABORATORS

After occupying Norway, the Germans had tried to gain support from the Norwegians by creating a puppet government that was headed by the leader of the Norwegian National Socialist Party, Vidkun Quisling. This action, however, resulted in a backlash against Quisling and his party. Quisling's government was replaced by an administrative council led by German commissioner Josef Terboven. Members of the council consisted of Norwegian collaborators who, after the war, were punished for treason.

Left: Norwegian diplomat Vidkun Quisling (*left*) and Nazi leader Heinrich Himmler (*right*) met during the time that Quisling was head of the puppet government set up in Norway by the Nazis in World War II.

Left: The German heavy water plant in Telemark is one site where Norway's resistance movement proved its strength during the German occupation in World War II.

Outwitting Germany's Nuclear Ambitions

The Germans set up a heavy water plant in Telemark. They had planned to use the heavy water, a substance that can cool nuclear reactors, to assist them in making an atomic bomb.

Aware of the Germans' plan, Norway and Britain prepared a mission to thwart the invaders. On February 16, 1943, a British-trained group from the Norwegian resistance crossed a gorge to the heavy water plant, where they laid explosives. The daring saboteurs fled before the explosives went off, but when they exploded the facility was severely disabled.

After several attacks, the Germans were discouraged enough to abandon the plant in Telemark, deciding instead to move the stock of heavy water back to Germany. The resistance then put a time bomb on the boat that was to carry the heavy water. The boat was blown up, and the Germans never reached their goal of manufacturing an atomic bomb.

Below: Norway's successful effort in shutting down the heavy water plant in Telemark was dramatized in the 1965 film *The Heroes of Telemark*, starring Kirk Douglas.

The Royal Family

A New Kingdom

After being united with Sweden for ninety-one years, Norway became an independent nation in 1905. Because of the unions with Denmark and then Sweden, Norway had not had a king of its own since Haakon VI died in 1380. Thus, Norway asked Prince Carl of Denmark to be the new king of Norway. He was young, and his bloodline was impressive.

Although Prince Carl was willing to take up the role, he asked for a vote to be held to ensure that the Norwegian people wanted him as their king. Norway held a national vote, and the result strongly favored his accession to the throne. On November 18, 1905, Prince Carl was elected king by the Storting. To continue the Norwegian royal lineage, he took the Old Norse name of Haakon and became Haakon VII of Norway.

A Beloved Monarchy

With a new name and a new throne, King Haakon VII began a reign that lasted through the two world wars. His strength and refusal to give in to the Germans was instrumental in forging a strong resistance movement in Norway. At the end of the war in 1945, he returned from hiding to Norway.

Left: Norwegians at the Trøndelag Folk Museum in Trøndheim stop to greet the royal family, who were there in 1997 to celebrate the sixtieth birthdays of the king and queen.

King Haakon's son, King Olav V, ruled Norway from 1957 to 1991. Norwegians liked his calm manner and his willingness to be like other citizens. He was even spotted skiing outside of Oslo without any bodyguards — something uncommon for many European royal families.

King Olav's son, Harald V, ascended the throne in 1991 and is the present king of Norway. Conservation of the environment is his passion, and he was president of the Norwegian branch of the World Wildlife Fund before becoming king. His wife, Queen Sonja, was a Norwegian commoner who became the country's first Norwegian-born queen when Harald V became king.

Royal Weddings

In December 2000, Mette-Marit Hoiby, the crown prince's fiancée, made her first official appearance with the crown prince at the Nobel Peace Prize ceremony, held at Oslo City Hall. Crown Prince Haakon married Hoiby on August 25, 2001, in Oslo Cathedral. On May 24, 2002, Crown Princess Martha Louise exchanged wedding vows with Norwegian author Ari Behn in Nidaros Cathedral.

Above: **Princess Martha Louise and author Ari Behn exchange rings on their wedding day in 2002.**

Below: **Both the crown prince (*right*) and the crown princess have chosen commoners as their spouses.**

The Sami

The Sami make up the largest minority group in Norway. Living primarily in Finnmark, the northernmost region of Norway, they are known for herding reindeer. Sami people are also found in the northernmost parts of Sweden, Finland, and Russia.

From a Nomadic to a Sedentary Lifestyle

The ancestors of the Sami were nomads who, when the polar ice cap retreated north, moved to northern Scandinavia. Descendants of the Sami continued their nomadic lifestyle in this new region, following herds of reindeer. As time went by, they domesticated the reindeer. Eventually, some Sami became less nomadic, settling in one place as hunters or fishermen.

The Norwegian Sami

The *Sameting* (SAW-meh-teeng), the Parliament of the Sami, serves the community by bringing Sami issues to the Storting. The Sami, however, were not always represented in government. Beginning in the mid-1800s, the Sami were encouraged to give up

LANGUAGE

Presently, more than half of the Sami population speaks Saami, in addition to Norwegian.

Left: Two Sami men from Finnmark take a break in their tent from herding reindeer.

their traditional ways and language in order to integrate fully into Norwegian society. There was even a time when land could not be sold to them because they did not speak Norwegian.

Since 1966, the identity of the Sami has been protected under Article 27 of the United Nations International Covenant on Civil and Political Rights. By the mid-1970s, Saami, the language of the Sami, was taught to children in Sami schools.

Above: **Although the reindeer remains an important part of Sami culture, less than 10 percent of the Sami in Norway today herd reindeer.**

Common Occupations Today

Today, the Sami work in fishing, agriculture, the service industry, and trade. They also make handicrafts. Reindeer-herding is still an important part of Sami life, and this practice is now organized to prevent overgrazing of the land.

Interaction with other Sami Communities

Sami people living in Norway, Sweden, Finland, and Russia keep in touch with each other. In recent years, communication with the Sami in Russia has improved. Although cultural freedom has increased over the past century, the main issue for the Sami people is to maintain their traditional livelihoods and ways of life.

RELIGION

The traditional Sami religion is shamanism. The main belief of shamanism is that spirits talk to special priests, or shamans. In Norway today, Lutheranism is the dominant religion among the Sami people.

Saving Norway's Lakes and Oceans

Air Pollution

The chief environmental issue facing Norway's lakes and rivers is acid rain. Acid rain is rain that contains high concentrations of sulfuric and nitric acids, which are produced by air pollution. Fish mortality as a result of acid rain is not a new phenomenon. Fish stocks were probably already dying in the early 1900s, but it was not until the 1950s and 1960s that people realized that this depletion was caused by acid rain.

In Norway, the southern counties have been badly hit; approximately one-third of the lakes are seriously affected. Presently, the northern parts of Norway are mostly unaffected by acid rain. The eastern region of Finnmark, which receives pollution from Russia, is the exception.

Because acid rain is a major environmental concern, Norway has been a supporter of international emission standards that are aimed at reducing air pollution.

ACID RAIN

Cars and industrial plants burn fossil fuels, such as gas and oil, which emit both sulfur dioxide and nitrogen oxide. These gases combine with water vapor in the atmosphere to form sulfuric acid and nitric acid. The resulting rain that falls from the clouds is acidic. Because clouds travel, much of the acid rain in Norway originates from Britain and the rest of Europe.

Left: Since most of the nation's energy needs are met through hydroelectric power, Norway releases little air pollution into the atmosphere. Although hydroelectric power is environmentally safe, dams like this one displace fish from their habitats.

Above: **Norwegians, especially residents living in the coastal districts, are highly dependent on the nation's tributaries.**

Overfishing

The oceans surrounding Norway have historically been excellent areas for fishing. With the advancement of fishing technology in the 1960s, huge catches were common, and the fishing industry in Norway was generally a free-for-all. By the 1970s, the size of the catches had declined, and the herring species was almost wiped out.

In 1977, to stop overfishing, the Norwegian government established a 200-nautical mile (322-nautical km) protected zone off the Norwegian mainland. Norway now makes fishing quota agreements with the European Union, Russia, Iceland, Greenland, and Poland, to ensure that the fishing industry does not deplete the oceans of their stocks.

Diseases

Another environmental concern is caused by aquaculture, or the fish-farming industry. Because fish in these farms are confined to small areas, there is a greater possibility that they will contract diseases. The concern is that some of these diseased fish might escape to the sea and spread diseases to the wild fish stocks.

Traditional Clothes

Bunader

The traditional costume of Norway is called the bunad. The word *bunad* is an old Norse word that means "clothing." Bunader were fairly common as everyday outfits in some regions of Norway until World War II. Now, they are typically worn on special occasions such as national holidays and weddings. In Norway, there are hundreds of different bunader, each representing a different region.

The Woman's Bunad

A woman's bunad consists of a full dark skirt, an apron, a silk scarf, and a bodice. Married women may also wear short capes. The costumes come in striking colors and have elaborate embroidery. Differences in embroidery correspond to the different periods in Norwegian history. One other important part of the outfit is the silver jewelry that complements the ensemble. The jewelry is worn on blouses, bodices, and skirts. Black leather shoes with silver buckles and dark stockings are commonly worn with the outfit. Almost every Norwegian woman has a bunad that has been usually passed down from mother to daughter.

Left: **Bunader are either made in the style of current folk costumes or are based on old folk costumes that have been preserved. Because much of the work is done by hand, each bunad is unique.**

The Man's Bunad

A man's bunad consists of a jacket worn over a vest, a cap, dark breeches, and socks. Breeches and jackets are usually made of fine black cloth, and the jacket is worn open to show the decorative silver brass buttons on the vest. Men do not wear their bunader as often as women wear theirs.

Above: These brilliant Norwegian sweaters have intricate designs and pretty buttons. More importantly, they help keep people warm during cold weather.

Norwegian Sweaters

Norwegian sweaters were born of necessity due to the country's cold winter temperature. Symbolic patterns are often used in sweater design. For example, one sweater pattern features the Gothic arches from the Nidaros Cathedral in Trøndheim. Contrasting colors — such as white on black or blue, or black or blue on white — are often used to make symmetrical designs. Some sweaters may have buttons or clasps on the front that are made of pewter and often feature intricate designs. Hats and mittens are also made using the same designs as sweaters.

Valorous Vikings

The Vikings derived their name from the word for pirates in the early Scandinavian languages. Formidable fighters, they razed and looted entire villages throughout Europe from A.D. 800 to A.D. 1100 and were possibly the most feared and barbaric warriors of their time. Within Scandinavia, however, the Vikings were a peaceful people. Mostly farmers, Viking men, sometimes called Norsemen, left Scandinavia due to overpopulation.

Viking Homesteads

The Vikings' homes were made of timber and roofed with turf. Viking settlements were centered around a longhouse, a barn-like structure where the family lived. Other buildings included storehouses and workshops, which were usually situated close to water, the community's main mode of transportation.

Innovators in Sea Transportation

The Vikings were excellent seamen. They were innovators in boat designs and excellent ocean navigators. Until the Viking period,

EXPLORERS

Originating from Norway, Sweden, and Denmark, Vikings who inhabited Norway are believed to have been the first discoverers of Greenland, in A.D. 985, and North America, in A.D. 1000.

ERIC THE RED

Eric the Red (950–1001), a Norwegian Viking explorer, was the first European to explore Greenland and set up a colony there. His son, Leif Eriksson (975–1020), is believed to be one of the first Europeans to reach North America; Eriksson landed in North America in around A.D. 1000.

Left: This Viking longboat is housed in the Viking Museum in Oslo.

boats had been primitive and not very seaworthy. The Vikings invented a sturdy type of vessel, called a longboat, that could cut through deep seas and travel easily into shallow waters. Using longboats, they could land on shores with great speed during surprise attacks and then retreat before any retaliation.

Viking raids decreased when the Vikings converted to Christianity. By A.D. 1100, the raids ceased altogether.

Although fearsome, the Vikings were indirectly responsible for promoting trade throughout Europe. In addition, the design of the useful Viking longboat was adopted by other Western explorers, making further sea exploration possible and opening up cultures that had been unknown until then.

Above: **Odin (*left*) was the chief Norse God. Before the Vikings were Christianized, they believed that it was a great honor to die in battle because they believed their spirits would join Odin in Asgard. Thor (*right*), Odin's son, is easily recognized by his hammer which he used to cause thunder and lightning.**

Viking Words

Vikings raided and settled in large areas of Eastern and Western Europe, leaving traces of their presence that are still felt today. Some of the Viking colonies established in Britain still have Viking names, such as Brimtoft, Grimsby, Thoresby, and Langtoft. Other words that are derived from the Viking language are "welcome," "egg," and "sister."

WIVES OF VIKINGS

As the men left their settlements for long periods of time, Viking women took on more responsibility than was common at the time and were expected to manage farms by themselves.

Vigeland's Artistry

Adolf Gustav Vigeland is Norway's most famous sculptor. His greatest artistic achievement — and one of Norway's major attractions — is Vigeland Park in Oslo.

Gustav Vigeland was born on April 11, 1869, to a farming family in Mandal, Norway. As a child, he showed great talent as a carver, and, at the age of fourteen, he was apprenticed to a woodcarver in Kristiana. After the death of his father, he had to return to Mandal to take care of his family. Unable to give up his dream, Vigeland continued to read about the arts and sketch statues. When he turned nineteen, he finally returned to the capital. Brynjulf Bergslien, a sculptor in Kristiana, was impressed by Vigeland's sketches and offered him training. A year later, in 1889, Vigeland held his first exhibition.

Vigeland also trained in Denmark, France, Germany, and Italy. He started out working in the classical genre, and his early works, mostly busts and reliefs, are found in the Vigeland Museum in Oslo. From 1897 to 1902, Vigeland worked on restoring the Nidaros Cathedral in Trøndheim. There he carved gargoyles to replace sculptures that had been damaged over time. Later, he was drawn to the more naturalistic movements in art.

Above: **Standing in the center of Vigeland Park, Vigeland's monolith is carved from a single piece of stone quarried from the Iddefjorden in southeastern Norway.**

Left: **The statues in Vigeland Park often portray human figures in candid poses.**

Vigeland's Monumental Achievement

The City of Kristiana recognized Vigeland's talents and, in 1902, provided him with a studio. In return, Vigeland donated all his works, including his original models and sketches, to the city. For Vigeland, this was a dream come true, and, in 1924, he began working on the sculptures that are now displayed in Vigeland Park.

Today, Vigeland Park is filled with almost two hundred works made of granite and bronze, that together include more than six hundred figures. The sculptures are often entwined human forms, lizards, or other animals. Standing at a height of 57 feet (17 m), a stone monolith is located in the center of the park. The monolith features carvings of 121 entangled bodies that seem to be on a quest for the top. To complete this giant pillar, three carvers had to work daily from 1929 to 1943. Gustav Vigeland worked on the park figures for almost twenty years before passing away in 1943.

Above: **The elaborate gates of Vigeland Park were also designed by Gustav Vigeland.**

Women in Norway

During the Viking era, women gained higher status in society, as they were expected to run the farms while their husbands were away. In modern times, Norway has strived to improve women's rights, and the nation is now considered at the forefront of promoting equality for women.

Women in Politics

One major reason for Norway's reputation as a leader in women's rights is the success of women in Norwegian politics. Gro Harlem Brundtland, who was elected in 1981, was both Norway's first female prime minister and the country's youngest prime minister. In the 1997 general election, 36 percent of the representatives elected to the Storting were women.

Women's Rights

Norway instituted the Gender Equality Act in 1978. This act promotes equal opportunities for women at work. One ruling made under the act is that only hiring for actors and models can be gender-specific. In order to enforce the rulings made under the act, Norway's government includes a Gender Equality Ombud.

ASSISTANCE

More than 70 percent of women in Norway have paid employment outside of the home, with many women choosing to work part-time. For working mothers and their families, a large amount of financial assistance comes in the form of family allowances and daycare programs that are provided by the Norwegian government.

Left: Gro Harlem Brundtland was the first woman prime minister in Norway. A trained physician, she is now director of the World Health Organization.

SAMI WOMEN

Gába, a women's magazine, focuses on women's issues within Sami communities. The magazine includes interviews, short stories, and poems. The Sami NissonForum is a formal network that holds seminars to aid Sami women in various areas, such as teaching them how to use technology such as the Internet and e-mail.

Left: Grete Waitz has retired from professional running, but continues to run about 40 miles (64 km) each week.

An Inspiration to Women Athletes

Norwegian long-distance runner Grete Waitz was the world's leading female runner from the late 1970s to the 1980s. In 1979, she became the first woman to complete the New York Marathon in 2 1/2 hours and went on to win the New York Marathon nine times. Waitz broke several records and remains an active promoter of women's sports. The 4.3-mile (7-km) Grete Waitz Marathon is held annually in Oslo.

Still Room for Improvement

The average wage for women in Norway is still significantly lower than for their male counterparts. Most women typically enter the workforce in traditionally female fields, such as nursing or social welfare. As in other modern societies, the sharing of housework within the family has improved in recent years, although women still typically do more housework than men.

Although there is definite room for improvement, women in Norway have made important steps toward equality throughout the years.

DATES TO REMEMBER

Some important years in women's liberation in Norway include 1882, when women were allowed to go to college; 1903, when the University of Oslo awarded the first doctorate earned by a woman; and 1913, when women in Norway gained the right to vote.

RELATIONS WITH NORTH AMERICA

Relations between Norway and North America have always been strong. The first contact between the two continents happened when Leif Eriksson set foot on North America a thousand years ago, during the Viking era. Eight hundred years later, nearly a third of Norway's population left for North America in search of a better life. During World War II, Norway was an important ally of the United States and Canada. When the Norwegian royal family avoided capture by the Germans, the Norwegian king and crown prince stayed in London. The Norwegian queen and the

Opposite: **Dressed in a bunad, an American girl of Norwegian descent puts an arm around her grandmother while holding a photograph of her ancestors.**

rest of the royal family stayed in the United States during the war, by invitation of U.S. president Franklin D. Roosevelt.

North Americans of Norwegian descent have become valuable members of the North American society, succeeding in sports, entertainment, and politics. Many Norwegians in Norway have relatives in the United States and Canada, and this link helps to foster a strong and healthy relationship between the three nations. As members of the U.N. and NATO, the United States, Canada, and Norway have worked together to help establish peace in war-torn areas of the world.

Above: **King Harald V of Norway pays an official visit to Canada in May 2002.**

Three Nations and their Common Goals

Norway, the United States, and Canada were close allies during World War II, in which the three fought against Nazi Germany. As founding members of NATO, all three countries continued to promote a stable world environment after the war. More than sixty thousand Norwegians have served in over thirty U.N. operations since 1948. Both the United States and Norway participated in the U.N. operations in Bosnia and Kosovo. Today, the U.N. has about 1,600 Norwegian personnel.

Norway, the United States, and Canada share the commitment of preserving equality, freedom, and basic human rights. The Norwegian constitution was also greatly influenced by the United States Declaration of Independence. The two countries' constitutions have one other thing in common: they are the world's two oldest constitutions still in use today.

Diplomatic relations between Norway and Canada began in 1942, during the trying times of World War II. Canada provided a training camp for Norway's military during the war against Germany. Over three thousand Norwegian soldiers, sailors, and airmen were trained in Canada's "Little Norway," which is located in Muskoka, Ontario.

Below: **Military leaders from the United States (*left*) and Norway (*right*) meet for a NATO discussion in 1949.**

Current Relations with North America

Norwegian prime minister Kjell Magne Bondevik met U.S. president George W. Bush at the White House on December 5, 2001. The two discussed issues such as the Middle East and the terrorist attacks on the United States. Immediately following the events of September 11, 2001, Norway offered its support to the United States through channels in NATO. Norway helped the United States by sending crime scene experts to the crash sites and by providing intelligence assistance. The country also supported NATO operations that secured U.S. skies.

On May 8, 2002, Norway's King Harald V and Queen Sonja were invited to Canada by Governor General Adrienne Clarkson. They visited Queen's Park in Toronto and the location that used to be known as "Little Norway. " The king and queen also attended business forums during their state visit.

Above: **King Harald V and Queen Sonja of Norway visit "Little Norway" during their state visit to Canada.**

Trade Relations with Canada

Canada and Norway signed the Trade and Economic Cooperation Agreement (TECA) in December 1997. The agreement is aimed at enhancing economic relations and encouraging investment.

Today, Norway is Canada's fifth largest trading partner in Europe. Canadian exports to Norway include primary products such as ore, aircraft, and aircraft components, while Canada imports seafood, machinery, and petroleum from Norway. The construction of the Hibernia oil field off the coast of Newfoundland was carried out with technological assistance from concrete firms in Norway. Currently, Canada and Norway are among the countries that attend conferences on oil and gas production that focus on environmental issues.

The Norwegian-Canadian Chamber of Commerce and the Norwegian Trade Council in Ontario assist potential and existing small- to medium-sized business ventures between the two countries. Norwegian companies are now emerging in Canada. For example, Fabcon Canada, which was established in Canada in 1991, is a Norwegian firm that provides specially trained workers for the oil and gas industries.

Below: **The Hibernia field, off the coast of Newfoundland, is the world's first Arctic offshore oil development. Oil workers live on a structure near the oil field, where they work to extract and transport the crude oil and natural gas.**

Left: **President George W. Bush (***right***) met Norwegian prime minister Kjell Magne Bondevik (***left***) in December 2001 at the White House in Washington, D.C.**

Trade Relations with the United States

The United States is Norway's largest trading partner outside Europe. More than 7 percent of Norwegian exports go to the United States. Some of the major imports from the United States to Norway are computer technology and automobiles. The United States is Norway's largest foreign investor, and U.S. investment is largely devoted to the lucrative petroleum industry in Norway.

The Norwegian Seafood Export Council's administrative office in the United States is located in Boston, Massachusetts. It approves exporters of seafood to the United States, provides information on the fishing industry in Norway, and also actively markets Norwegian seafood to Americans.

Norway's trade relations with the United States have been tested in recent years over the issue of whaling and the exporting of whale products. Norway has maintained its right to a limited harvest of the minke whale. The United States is against whaling, and various U.S. presidents have been cautious when handling this issue so as to avoid damaging the friendly diplomatic relations between the two countries.

The First European in North America

About one thousand years ago, Leif Eriksson, son of Norwegian Viking Eric the Red, sailed from Greenland to Newfoundland, Canada. Leif Eriksson is believed to be the first person from Europe to visit North America.

The Viking sagas relate that Leif built a temporary settlement in a region he called Vinland. He named the place "Vinland," or the "Land of Wine," for the grapes that were found growing in the forests.

Remains of this settlement have been found at L'Anse aux Meadows in Newfoundland, Canada. In 1960, Helge Ingstad (1899–2001), a Norwegian archaeologist, and his wife, Anne Stine, located the legendary Vinland at L'Anse aux Meadows after carefully reading the sagas of Vinland. An international team of experts assisted the couple in finding the remains of several structures and artifacts, all of which had distinct Viking designs.

Below: **Norwegian archaeologist Helge Ingstad (*right*) and his wife, Anne Stine, take a break from their fieldwork at L'Anse aux Meadows.**

Today, the ruins at L'Anse aux Meadows are a National Historic Site in Canada as well as a UNESCO World Heritage Site. Parks Canada, a government organization that preserves the natural heritage of Canada, manages the site.

Left: I Remember Mama (1948) dramatizes the lives of twentieth-century Norwegian immigrants in the United States. The film was adapted from the 1943 autobiography of Kathryn Forbes, titled *Mama's Bank Account.*

From Norway to the United States

The first organized emigration from Norway to the United States occurred in 1825, when Cleng Peerson, a Norwegian Quaker from Tysvær, led a group of fifty-two passengers aboard a kind of ship called a sloop and embarked on a journey to New York. The promise of cheap and fertile land in the United States, and factors such as drought, high land prices, political instability, and massive population growth in Norway motivated the emigrants to search for a better home in the New World. These first emigrants who traveled on the sloop, which was called *Restoration*, are now known as the "Sloopers."

The Sloopers first settled in Kendall Township, located in western New York state. They also established settlements in Minnesota, Iowa, and Indiana. Most of them were farmers. As these immigrants settled in the Midwest, they welcomed and assisted other immigrants from Norway. This marked the start of a mass exodus in which almost one-third of the Norwegian population migrated to North America.

MASSIVE MIGRATION TO NORTH AMERICA

So many people have moved from Norway to North America that Norway is second only to Ireland in terms of the percentage of the nation's population that emigrated to North America.

COMMON TRADES

Aside from farming and fishing, early Norwegian immigrants to the United States worked as carpenters and construction workers.

Norwegians in the United States Today

Almost 52 percent of all Norwegian-Americans reside in the Midwest. Minnesota has the largest number of Norwegian-Americans, followed by Wisconsin. Approximately 17 percent of the population of Minnesota is Norwegian-American. Two other states that have a significant Norwegian-American population are Washington and California. Other distinctive Norwegian communities can be found in Seattle, Minneapolis, Chicago, and Brooklyn, New York. Today, the United States has more than 4.5 million people of Norwegian descent; this number is larger than the population in Norway.

Several associations in the United States have been established for the Norwegian-American community. The American-Scandinavian Foundation is located on New York's Park Avenue. A non-profit organization, the foundation promotes cultural exchange between the United States and Scandinavian countries, including Norway. It publishes magazines, including the *Scandinavian Review*, that give an insight into the commerce, politics, and societies in Scandinavian countries. The foundation also holds language courses, film screenings, lectures, and exhibitions about Scandinavia.

NEWSPAPERS

While the popularity of most Norwegian-American newspapers has declined in recent years, the *Western Viking*, in Seattle, is still being published every week.

Left: These early Norwegian immigrants arrived in Winneshick County, Iowa, in around 1860.

Norwegians in Canada

Beginning in the late 1840s, traveling via ships and then rail, Norwegians began to arrive in parts of Canada. Most of them traveled from Quebec to Toronto and then crossed the border into the United States. Some of these migrants remained in Lower Canada and settled in the Gaspe Peninsula. Others made their homes in Sherbrooke, Quebec. The initial number of Norwegian immigrants in Canada, however, was small compared to that of the United States.

Today, Canada has about 350,000 citizens of Norwegian descent. These immigrants have made their homes both in the prairie provinces of Manitoba, Saskatchewan, and Alberta and in cities such as Toronto, Montreal, and Vancouver.

The Scandinavian Community Center, located in British Columbia, has a Norwegian House Society, which organizes activities such as Constitution Day celebrations and Midsummer festivals for Norwegian-Canadians.

The Royal Norwegian Embassy in Ottawa devotes itself to promoting cultural and commercial ties between Norway and Canada. Together with the Association for the Advancement of Scandinavian Studies in Canada, the Norwegian embassy provides study grants for Canadians who wish to travel to Norway for academic pursuits.

Above: **The Royal Canadian Mint produced a five dollar coin to commemorate the thousandth anniversary of the arrival of the Vikings in North America.**

A Skating Star

Sonja Henie (1912–1969) was a Hollywood movie star and one of the most popular celebrities of the 1930s and 1940s. Born in Oslo, Henie started skating at the age of six. At the age of ten, she won her first Norwegian national figure skating championship. In 1927, Henie won an international skating championship and went on to hold the world champion title for the next ten years. Henie represented Norway in the Winter Olympics four times, winning the gold medal in figure skating in 1928, 1932, and 1936.

In March 1936, immediately following her third Olympic gold medal, Henie signed a five-year contract with the American film company Twentieth Century Fox. Her first film was *One in a Million* (1937), which was an immediate hit at the box office. Henie's acting career soared, and she entertained both American audiences and viewers around the world for years to come. The roles she played always highlighted her skating talent, and, by the time of her death in 1969, Henie had starred in twelve Hollywood films.

AN INSPIRATION

Henie influenced modern figure skating by being the first figure skater to combine skating and ballet moves. Her short skirt and white skates were also new looks that are still popular among today's skaters.

Left: Norwegian-born Sonja Henie became one of the biggest Hollywood stars in the 1930s and 1940s. In 1941, she became an American citizen.

Liv Ullman (1938–)

Another famous Norwegian is actress and director Liv Ullman. She was nominated for Academy Awards for best actress for her roles in the movies *The Emigrants* (1972) and *Face to Face* (1976). Other films that Ullman acted in include *Persona* (1966) and *40 Carats* (1967).

Ullman received critical acclaim for directing the 1995 film adaptation of Sigrid Undset's Nobel Prize-winning novel *Kristin Lavransdatter*. In 1980, the actress-turned-director became the first female Goodwill Ambassador for the United Nations Children's Fund (UNICEF).

STAGE DEBUT

Liv Ullman made her Broadway debut in a 1975 production of *A Doll's House.* The play was written by the well-loved Norwegian playwright Henrik Ibsen.

An American "Viking"

Jan Stenerud (1942–) is a Norwegian-born American who played professional football for nineteen seasons with the Kansas City Chiefs, Green Bay Packers, and the Minnesota Vikings. Stenerud incorporated a soccer style kick, often kicking the football from the side, instead of straight-on, as was typical in his day. His style was unconventional, but Stenerud enjoyed great success. He retired with 1,699 points and still ranks as one of professional football's highest scorers. In his first year of eligibility, 1991, Stenerud's name was enshrined in the Pro Football Hall of Fame.

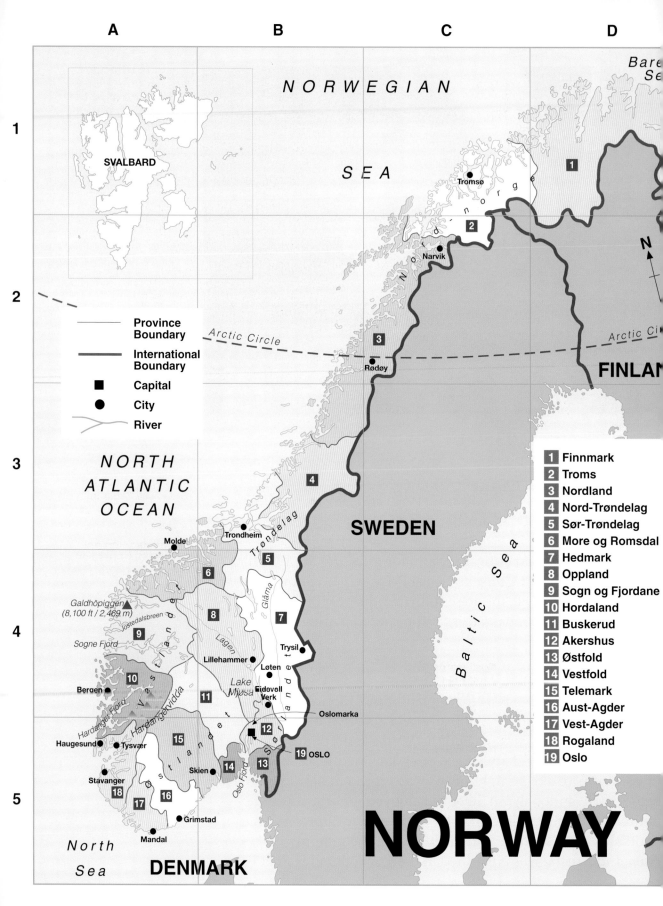

A   B   C   D

NORWEGIAN

Bare
Se

1

SVALBARD

SEA

Tromsø

1

2

Narvik

2

Province
Boundary

International
Boundary

■ Capital

● City

～ River

Arctic Circle

3

Arctic Ci

Rødøy

FINLAN

*NORTH
ATLANTIC
OCEAN*

4

SWEDEN

Trondheim

Molde

5

6

Galdhöpiggen
(8,100 ft / 2,469 m)

Jostedalsbreen

8

7

Baltic Sea

1 Finnmark
2 Troms
3 Nordland
4 Nord-Trøndelag
5 Sør-Trøndelag
6 More og Romsdal
7 Hedmark
8 Oppland
9 Sogn og Fjordane
10 Hordaland
11 Buskerud
12 Akershus
13 Østfold
14 Vestfold
15 Telemark
16 Aust-Agder
17 Vest-Agder
18 Rogaland
19 Oslo

9

Sogne Fjord

Lagen

Trysil

Lillehammer

4

Løten

Bergen

10

Lake
Mjøsa

Eidsvoll
Verk

11

Oslomarka

Hardanger Fjord

Haugesund

Tysvær

15

12

19 OSLO

Stavanger

18

16

17

14

Skien

13

Grimstad

Mandal

5

*North
Sea*

DENMARK

NORWAY

Above: This aerial view shows how close some of Norway's towns are to its coast.

Akershus (county)
   B4–B5
Arctic Circle A1–D2
Aust-Agder (county)
   A5–B5

Barents Sea D1
Bergen (city) A4
Buskerud (county)
   A4–B5

Eidsvoll Verk B4
Finland C1–D5
Finnmark (county)
   A1–D2

Galhöpiggen A4
Glåma (river) B4–B5
Grimstad A5

Hardanger Fjord A4–A5
Hardangervidda
   (mountain range) A4
Haugesund A5
Hedmark (county) B4–B5
Hordaland (county)
   A4–A5

Jostedalsbreen
   (glacier) A4

Lagen (river) A4–B4
Lake Mjøsa B4
Lillehammer B4
Løten B4

Mandal A5
Molde A4
More og Romsdal
   (county) A3–B4

Narvik C2
Nordland (county)
   B2–C3
Nord-Norge (region)
   B3–D1
Nord-Trøndelag
   (county) B3
North Atlantic Ocean
   A4–B3
North Sea A5–B5
Norwegian Sea B2–C1

Oppland (county) A4–B5
Oslo B5
Oslo Fjord B5
Oslomarka B5
Østfold (county) B5
Østlandet (region)
   A4–B5

Rødøy C2
Rogaland (county) A5
Russia D1–D2

Skien B5
Sogne Fjord A4
Sogn og Fjordane
   (county) A4
Sørlandet (region)
   B4–B5
Sør-Trøndelag (county)
   B3–B4
Stavanger A5
Svalbard A1–B1
Sweden B5–C1

Telemark (county)
   A4–B5
Troms (county) C2–D1
Tromsø C1
Trøndelag (region)
   B3–B4
Trondheim B3
Trysil B4
Tysvær A5

Vest-Agder (county) A5
Vestfold (county) B5
Vestlandet (region)
   A5–B3

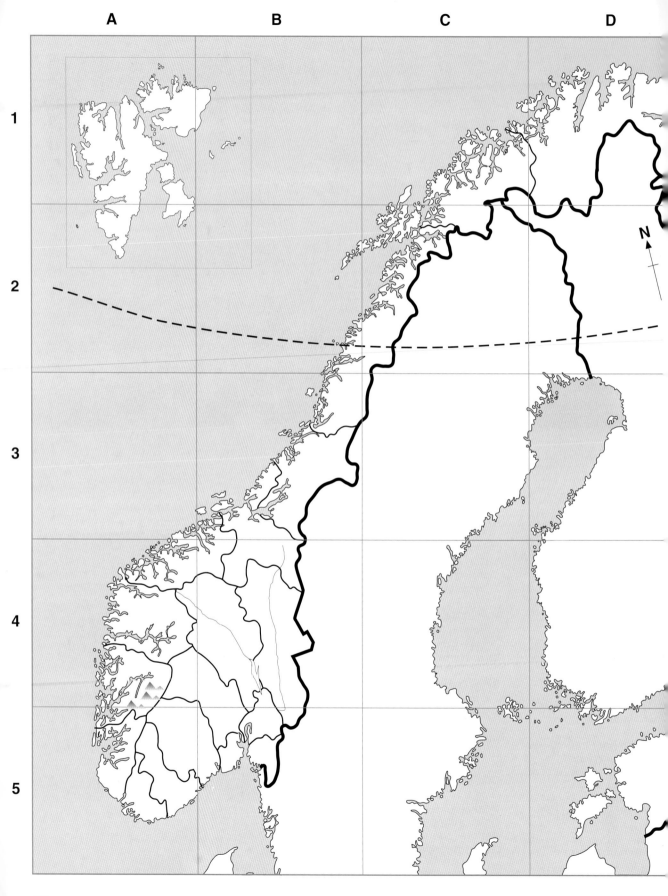

A   B   C   D

1

2

N

3

4

5

How Is Your Geography?

Learning to identify the main geographical areas and points of a country can be challenging. Although it may seem difficult at first to memorize the locations and spellings of major cities or the names of mountain ranges, rivers, deserts, lakes, and other prominent physical features, the end result of this effort can be very rewarding. Places you previously did not know existed will suddenly come to life when referred to in world news, whether in newspapers, television reports, other books and reference sources, or on the Internet. This knowledge will make you feel a bit closer to the rest of the world, with its fascinating variety of cultures and physical geography.

Used in a classroom setting, the instructor can make duplicates of this map using a copy machine. (PLEASE DO NOT WRITE IN THIS BOOK!) Students can then fill in any requested information on their individual map copies. Used one-on-one, the student can also make copies of the map on a copy machine and use them as a study tool. The student can practice identifying place names and geographical features on his or her own.

Above: **The grounds at Akershus Festning are well maintained by the government.**

Norway at a Glance

Official Name	Kingdom of Norway
Capital	Oslo
Official Language	Norwegian
Population	4,503,440 (2001 estimate)
Land Area	118,834 square miles (307,860 square km)
Regions	Nord-Norge, Østlandet, Sørlandet, Trøndelag, Vestlandet
Counties	Akershus, Aust-Agder, Buskerud, Finnmark, Hedmark, Hordaland, More og Romsdal, Nordland, Nord-Trøndelag, Oppland, Oslo, Østfold, Rogaland, Sogn og Fjordane, Sør-Trøndelag, Telemark, Troms, Vest-Agder, Vestfold
Highest Point	Galdhöppigen 8,100 feet (2,469 m)
Major Rivers	Glåma, Lagen
Major Cities	Oslo, Bergen, Trøndheim, Stavanger
Main Religion	Evangelical Lutheranism
National Anthem	*Ja, vi elsker dette landet* (Yes, we love this land)
Major Holidays	Easter week (March/April)
	Constitution Day (May 17)
	Midsummer's Eve (June 23)
	Christmas (December 24)
Imports	Chemicals, foodstuffs, and metals.
Exports	Petroleum and petroleum products, fish, machinery, and metal products
Currency	Krone (NOK 7.5 = U.S. $1 in 2002)

Opposite: Karl Johans Gate is the main street in Oslo. It runs from the central railroad to the Royal Palace.

Glossary

Norwegian Vocabulary

Allemannsretten (AWL-leh-mawns-rehtten): "every man's right"; a Norwegian law granting the right of public access.

Bokmål (BOOK-mohl): "Book Language"; Dano-Norwegian language.

bunader (BOO-nad-der): the traditional costume of Norway.

flatbrød (FLAWT-brohd): crispy, wafer-thin bread.

formiddagsmat (fawh-MIH-dawgs-mawt): a snack between breakfast and lunch.

fotball (FOOT-bawl): soccer.

frokost (FROOK-oost): breakfast.

gomme (GOO-meh): a sweet milk dish that is eaten with waffles.

hulder (HOOL-der): a female troll that can seduce a young man into marrying her.

Jul (YOOL): Christmas.

julegrøt (YOOL-eh-groht): rice pudding that contains one almond.

kveldsmat (keh-VELL-dis-mawt): a post-dinner evening meal.

Lagting (LAG-teeng): the upper house of Parliament.

Landsmål (LAWNDS-mohl): an early form of Nynorsk.

linje akevitt (LIN-yeh AWKE-vit): a liquor flavored with caraway seeds that has been transported across the equator.

lunsj (LOON-sh): lunch.

middag (MIH-dawg): lunch.

nisse (NIH-seh): a small, humanlike creature in Norwegian folklore that lives in barns.

nøkken (NOK-kehn): a type of troll that lives under waterfalls.

Nynorsk (NEE-nohrsk): New Norwegian.

Odelsting (OO-dels-teeng): the lower house of Parliament.

ringe Julen (REEN-geh YOOL-en): ringing in Christmas.

rommegrøt (ROHM-meh-groht): sour cream porridge.

rosemaling (ROO-seh-moh-ling): "rose painting"; a traditional form of Norwegian painting.

Samnorsk (SAWM-nohrsk): a unique Norwegian language that combines Bokmål and Nynorsk.

Sankthansaften (SAWNKT-hawns-awf-tehn): Midsummer's Eve.

Storting (STOOR-teeng): the Norwegian legislative body.

Syttende Mai (SIH-tehn-deh MEYE-ee): May 17, Norway's Constitution Day.

Saami Vocabulary

joik (YOYK): a type of yodeling that is common in Sami folk music.

Sameting (SAW-meh-teeng): the Sami legislative body.

English Vocabulary

apothecary: a pharmacist.

aquaculture: the cultivation of aquatic animals or plants.

asylum seekers: refugees seeking protection or shelter granted by another country or embassy, after being forced to leave their own countries for political, religious, or cultural reasons.

backlash: a strong negative reaction following a social or political change.

breeches: knee-length trousers.

bullion: gold in the form of bars or ingots.

canonized: declared officially as a saint.

collaborators: people who cooperate with an enemy nation, especially with an enemy occupying their country.

confirmed: accepted formally as a member of a Christian church at a special ceremony.

constitution: the system of principles by which a nation or country is governed.

deterred: discouraged; put off.

dialects: regional varieties of a language that have distinctive vocabulary, pronunciations, and grammar rules.

dialogue: discussion in order to resolve disagreements or problems.

dirigible: a light, self-propelled air craft.

dissolution: separation into parts.

disparity: difference.

exodus: a mass departure or emigration.

fjords: narrow inlets of the sea between cliffs or steep slopes.

formidable: causing fear or dread.

genre: a particular style.

gorge: a narrow cleft or canyon with steep, rocky walls.

Great Depression: the period of world economic crisis that began with the U.S. stock market crash in 1929 and continued through most of the 1930s.

hail: to come or originate from.

homogeneous: composed of parts or elements that are similar or the same.

hydroelectric: related to the generation of electricity from water power.

looted: stole goods or valuables by open force, as in war.

lucrative: profitable; producing wealth.

mandatory: compulsory; obligatory.

monolith: a large column or statue made from a single block of stone.

neutrality: not taking part or assisting in a dispute between others.

nomadic: moving around from place to place.

pewter: a bluish-gray metal that is a mixture of tin and lead.

prominent: important or well known.

prophesy: foretell or predict.

razed: torn down.

reliefs: sculptures made from a flat surface on which the forms or figures are raised above the background.

saboteurs: people who deliberately destroy property, as to undermine a government or military effort.

sedentary: characterized by inactivity and lack of exercise.

slums: run-down parts of a city.

socialism: a system of government in which means of production are owned and controlled by the state.

tenets: opinions, principles, or doctrines that are believed to be true by members of a profession, group, or movement.

thwart: to oppose and prevent from accomplishing a purpose.

tributaries: streams that flow to a larger stream or other bodies of water.

turf: a layer of matted earth formed by grass and plant roots.

valorous: bold or determined in the face of danger.

virtuoso: highly skilled musical technique or performance.

More Books to Read

The Great Polar Adventure: The Journeys of Roald Amundsen. Great Explorers series. Andrew Langley (Chelsea House)

Norway. Cultures of the World series. Sakina Kagda and Rudolf Steiner (Benchmark Books)

Norway. Enchantment of the World series. Jean F. Blashfield (Children's Press)

Norway. Major World Nations series. Ralph Zickgraf (Chelsea House)

Norway. Modern Nations of the World series. Laurel Corona (Lucent Books)

The Sami of Northern Europe. First Peoples series. Deborah B. Robinson (Lerner)

Snow Treasure. Marie McSwigan (Scholastic Paperbacks)

The Troll With No Heart in His Body and Other Tales of Trolls from Norway. Lise Lunge-Larsen (Houghton Mifflin)

The Viking Explorers. Explorers of New Worlds series. Jim Gallagher (Chelsea House)

Videos

Song of Norway. (Anchor Bay Entertainment)

Travel the World: Scandinavia — Denmark, Sweden, and Norway. (Questar)

Video Visits — Norway — Nature's Triumph. (IVN Entertainment)

The Vikings. Foot Soldiers series. (A & E Home Video)

Web Sites

www.hf.uio.no/ibsensenteret/index_eng.html

www.norway.org

www.odin.dep.no/odin/engelsk/index-b-n-a.html

www.mnc.net/norway

Due to the dynamic nature of the Internet, some web sites stay current longer than others. To find additional web sites, use a reliable search engine with one or more of the following keywords to help you locate information about Norway. Keywords: *Roald Amundsen, fjords, Thor Heyerdahl, Henrik Ibsen, Oslo, rosemaling, Sami.*

Index

Aasen, Ivar 28
agriculture 6, 7, 10, 18, 48, 63, 81
Akershus Festning 55
Allied Forces 12, 13
American Declaration of Independence 76
American-Scandinavian Foundation 82
Amundsen, Roald 46
animals 9, 62, 63, 64, 65
architecture 22, 30, 31, 54
Arctic Circle 8, 48
Assembly of the League of Nations 15
Atlantic Ocean 6, 46

Behn, Ari 61
Bergen 7, 25, 31, 52, 57
Bergman, Ingmar 85
berries 9, 35
Bjørnson, Bjørnstjerne 29
Bondevik, Kjell Magne 77, 79
Brundtland, Gro Harlem 15, 72
bubonic plague 10, 11
Bull, Ole Bornemann 33
Bush, George W. 77, 79

Canada 46, 75, 76, 77, 78, 83
Charles XIII (Sweden) 11
children 21, 22, 24, 25, 26, 35, 38, 39, 45, 51
Christianity 10, 21, 26, 31, 38, 39, 63, 69
Clarkson, Adrienne 77
climate 8
Constitution Day 39, 44, 45
Crown Prince Haakon 61

Denmark 5, 10, 14, 25, 28, 44, 60, 68, 70

economy 5, 11, 13, 16, 18, 19, 23, 56
education 21, 24, 25, 26, 35, 73, 83
Eidsvoll Verk 44
Ellsworth, Lincoln 46
Eric the Red 68, 80
Eriksson, Leif 68, 75, 80
European Union (EU) 14, 19, 65

Festivals 38, 39
    Easter week 21, 38
    Midsummer's Eve 38
    Christmas 39, 52
Finland 6, 14, 20, 62, 63
Finnmark 20, 26, 62, 64
Finns 20, 21
fishing industry 7, 18, 63, 65, 81
fjords 5, 6, 7, 8, 9, 35, 48, 49
food 35, 39, 40, 41, 45
Forbes, Kathryn 81
forestry 7, 9, 18

Germany 19
Glåma River 6
government 16, 17, 22, 24, 25, 34, 43, 45, 58, 62, 65, 72
Great Depression 13
Greenland 15, 64, 68, 81
Grieg, Edvard 33, 53
Gulf Stream 8, 48

Harald I Fairhair 15
Hardanger fiddle 33
Haugesund 31
Heyerdahl, Thor 47
Hoiby, Mette-Marit 61
hydroelectricity 6, 7, 18, 57, 64

Ibsen, Henrik 29, 33, 52, 53, 85
Iceland 14, 29
immigrants 20, 21, 81
Ingstad, Helge 80
Italy 15, 70

Kalmar Union 11
King Olaf (Denmark) 11
King Oscar II (Sweden) 11
Kings
    Harald Hardraade 54
    Haraldsson, Olaf 10
    Haraldsson, Olaf II 15
    King Haakon V 55
    King Haakon VII (Prince Carl of Denmark) 12, 58, 60, 61
    King Harald V 61, 75, 77
    Olav V 26, 61
Kohn, Rosemarie 26
Koss, Olav Johann 36
Kristin Lavransdatter 29, 85

language 21, 23, 24, 28, 62, 63, 67, 82
L'Anse aux Meadows 80
Leipzig Conservatory 33
Lillehammer 36
Løten 32

Mandal 70
Meltzer, Frederik 5
mountains 6, 49
Munch, Edvard 32

Nansen, Fridtjof 15
National Insurance Act 14, 22, 43
Nazi government 13, 58, 59
Nobel prize 15, 24, 29

Nobile, Umberto 46
Nordic Council 14
North America 68, 75, 77, 80
North Atlantic Current 8, 37
North Atlantic Treaty
   Organization (NATO) 14,
   75, 76, 77
North Pole 46
Norse gods
   Frey 27
   Freya 27
   Odin 10, 27, 69
   Thor 27, 69
   Tyr 27
Norway spruce 9
Norwegian-Americans 75,
   82, 84, 85
Norwegian-Canadians 83
Norwegian Sea 6
Norwegian Seafood Export
   Council 79

Organization for Security and
   Cooperation in Europe
   (OSCE) 14
Oslo (Kristiana) 7, 12, 23, 25,
   26, 30, 31, 32, 34, 43, 47, 52,
   54, 55, 70, 71, 73, 84
Oslomarka 55
Østlandet 7

Pacific Ocean 46
petroleum 18, 19, 22, 43, 56,
   57, 78, 79
pollution 47, 56, 57, 64, 78
population 5, 20, 55, 57, 81
Prince Christian Frederik
   (Denmark) 44
Princess Martha Louise 61
Pro Football Hall of Fame 85

Queen Sonja 61, 77
Quisling, Vidkun 13, 58

resistance movement 13,
   43, 58, 59
Revold, Axel 32
Rolfsen, Alf 32
Roosevelt, Franklin D. 75
rosemaling 32
royal family 12
Russia 6, 15, 62, 63, 64, 65

Sami 20, 21, 25, 26, 29, 30,
   33, 43, 62, 63, 73
Scandinavia 5, 20, 28, 36,
   68, 82
Scandinavian Review 82
Scots pine 9
shamanism 63
Sørlandet 6, 7
South Pole 46
sports 34, 35, 73, 75
   fishing 35
   football 85
   handball 37
   hiking 34
   jazz ballet 37
   long-distance running 73
   orienteering 37
   sailing 34, 35, 37, 55
   skating 36, 84
   skiing 34, 35, 36, 37, 38, 55
   soccer 37, 45
   swimming 35, 37
   windsurfing 55
Stavanger 31
stave churches 22, 31
Stenerud, Jan 85
Stine, Anne 80
Svalbard 46
Sweden 5, 10, 14, 15, 16, 19,
   20, 44, 60, 62, 63, 68, 69

Telemark 19, 30, 58, 59
timber 6, 19, 30
traditional costumes 21, 23,
   38, 43, 45, 66, 67, 75

transportation 23, 68, 69
trolls 5, 50, 51, 53
Troms 20
Tromsø 25, 31, 37
Trøndelag 7
Trøndheim 7, 25, 31, 67
Trysil 36

Ullman, Liv 85
Undset, Sigrid 29, 85
United Kingdom 15, 26, 19,
   52, 56, 58, 64, 69
United Nations (U.N.) 5, 14,
   22, 75
United Nations Children's
   Fund (UNICEF) 85
United Nations Educational,
   Scientific, and Cultural
   Organization (UNESCO)
   31, 81
United States 13, 37, 75, 76,
   77, 79, 81, 82, 83

Valhalla 10, 27
Valkyries 27
Vestlandet 7
Vigeland, Adolf Gustav 30,
   55, 70, 71
Vikings 5, 10, 26, 27, 29, 31,
   38, 43, 46, 48, 54, 68, 69, 72,
   75, 83, 85
Vinland 81

Waitz, Grete 73
welfare system 5, 14, 20, 22,
   43, 56
Winter Olympic Games 36, 84
women 15, 16, 19, 20, 22, 26,
   43, 53, 69, 72, 73
World Health
   Organization 15
World War II 12, 13, 43, 44,
   58, 59, 75, 76
World Wildlife Fund 61